# GCSE
# Questions and Answers

Q&A

# INFORMATION TECHNOLOGY

KEY STAGE 4

**Steve Cushing**

Chief Examiner

SERIES EDITOR: BOB McDUELL

Letts EDUCATIONAL

# Contents

## HOW TO USE THIS BOOK

The aim of the *Questions and Answers* series is to provide you with help to do as well as possible in your examinations at GCSE or, in Scotland, at General and Credit levels. This book is based on the idea that an experienced examiner can give, through examination questions, sample answers and advice, the help students need to secure success and improve their grades.

The *Questions and Answers* series is designed to provide the following.

- **Introductory advice** on the different types of questions, and how to answer them to maximise your marks.
- Information about the other skills, apart from the recall of knowledge, that will be tested on examination papers. These are sometimes called **assessment objectives**.
- **Revision summaries** to remind you of the topics you will need to have revised in order to answer the examination questions.
- Many examples of **examination questions** arranged by topic, with spaces to fill in your answers, just as on an examination paper. Only try the questions after you have revised the topic thoroughly. Read the revision summary before attempting a question to double-check that you know the topic. It is best not to consult the answers before you try the questions.
- **Sample answers** to all of the questions.
- **Advice from examiners**. By using the experience of actual Chief Examiners, we are able to give advice on how you can improve your answers and avoid the most common mistakes.

This book is designed to help students studying for both short and full IT courses.

## THE IMPORTANCE OF USING QUESTIONS FOR REVISION

Past examination questions play an important part in revising for examinations. However, it is important not to start practising questions too early. Nothing can be more disheartening than trying to do a question which you do not understand because you have not mastered the topic. Therefore, it is important to have studied a topic thoroughly before attempting any questions on it.

How can past examination questions provide a way of preparing for the examination? It is unlikely that any question you try will appear in exactly the same form on the papers you are going to take. However, the examiner is restricted on what can be set because the questions must cover the whole syllabus and test certain assessment objectives. The number of totally original questions that can be set on any part of the syllabus is very limited and so similar ideas occur over and over again. Certainly, it will help you if the question you are trying to answer in an examination is familiar and if you know you have done similar questions before. This is a great boost for your confidence and confidence is what is required for examination success.

Practising examination questions will also highlight gaps in your knowledge and understanding which you can go back to and revise more thoroughly. It will also indicate the sorts of questions you can do well.

Attempting past questions will get you used to the type of language used in questions.

Finally, having access to answers, as you do in this book, will enable you to see clearly what is required by the examiner, how best to answer each question, and the amount of detail required. Attention to detail is a key aspect of achieving success at GCSE.

## EXAMINATION TECHNIQUE

Success in GCSE examinations comes from proper preparation and a positive attitude to the examination. This book is intended to help you overcome 'examination nerves' which often come from a fear of not being properly prepared. Examination technique is extremely important and certainly affects your performance. Remember the following basics.

- Read the questions carefully.
- Make sure that you watch the time carefully and complete the paper. It is no good answering one question well if you spend so long doing it that you do not answer another question at all.
- Read the rubric on the front of the examination paper carefully to make sure you know how many questions to attempt.
- Examination papers usually tell you how many marks are available for each answer. Take notice of this information, as the number of marks gives a guide to the importance of the question and often to the amount you ought to write.
- Check before the end of the examination that you have not missed any pages. Remember to turn over the last page, too.
- Remember to leave time to check through your work carefully.

## DIFFERENT TYPES OF EXAMINATION QUESTION

Examination boards use a range of types of question on GCSE IT papers. Some questions are based on the use of common software in a school context. Some examination boards like to extend this by placing the questions in an external context, and may issue a preparation sheet that states that the examination paper reflects the type of hardware and software that would be used in a doctor's surgery, an estate agent's or in a similar context. The important thing to remember is that whatever the context might be, the type of software and its features will be similar to that used in your school. Although some of the contexts mentioned may use mainframe computers, the examiners will presume that the software available reflects your experience using the school equipment.

Some questions will require one-word answers. As a rough guide, the number of marks allocated to a question will show you how much you are expected to write, but always read the question carefully to check what is expected of you. The number of lines marked on the examination paper will also give you a clue as to how much to write. The key to answering many examination questions comes from an appreciation of the command word – state/describe/explain/show/list/compare.

- **State**: this means give a brief answer, with no supporting evidence.
- **Describe**: you will need to show each stage and, wherever possible, use examples. This will be a longer answer.
- **Explain**: a short answer is required, with a clear explanation of why it is appropriate.
- **Show**: similar to describe. In some cases, a diagram or formula will be required.
- **List**: a list requires more than one idea, but a single word, or perhaps two words, will normally be enough for each idea.
- **Compare**: two items or more will be required, and you should explain the advantages and disadvantages of each.

Where examination questions ask for a full description, or ask for advantages and disadvantages, the examiner wants to see you develop your answer as you would in a short essay. You must; however, be careful not to pad out the answer with meaningless extra text.

Remember that each examiner has an enormous number of papers to read! For this sort of question, it is a good idea to plan your answer before you start to write, so that you fit the important information, in the right order, into the space on the examination paper.

Some questions will contain a number of parts, and these will be divided into sections labelled (a), (b), (c) and so on. The sections may in turn be divided into smaller sections labelled (i), (ii), (iii) and so on. This will help you to structure your answers.

Some questions will contain what examiners call a stem. This is where the question starts with a piece of information which you need in order to answer the question fully. An example of this would be 'Bill's garage is to use a database system for accounts details and customer billing.' All of the subsequent sections of the question will relate to this stem and it is worth reminding yourself of the stem each time you answer a section, particularly where a question goes over a page. You may find a number of stems in one question.

Check the requirements of your examination board and follow the instructions carefully. Get into the habit of laying out your work neatly and logically, and use the correct terminology wherever possible. You should try to answer all of the questions on the examination paper. Blank spaces cannot gain marks.

Examination questions do not all carry the same weight in terms of marks, so you need to be careful to spend the right amount of time on each question. For example, you should not spend more than one or two minutes on a one-mark question. Before you do the paper, it is worth checking how many marks are allocated to the examination by the board, and divide the total amount of time by the number of marks. A 60 minute examination paper with 120 marks would give you 30 seconds per mark awarded for each question, so if a whole question is worth 40 marks, you should reckon to spend 20 minutes on it. If you find yourself with time to spare at the end of the examination, you can always go back and check your answers.

Remember that, if you repeat answers in questions requiring a variety of responses, you will receive marks only once.

# 1 Computers and peripherals

REVISION SUMMARY

A computer is an automatic, programmable digital data processor. The computer processes digital data and produces some actions as a result. To make the computer function effectively, it requires an **input device** and an **output device**. These are known as peripherals. A computer is usually supplied with a keyboard, a mouse and a monitor. The keyboard and mouse are input devices, the monitor is an output device. It is normally desirable to connect the computer to a printer.

There are a number of types of computer, including mainframe, mini computers, personal computers (PCs), personal digital assistants, portable computers, palmtop and laptop computers, notebook, and multimedia and super computers. A PC, which has facilities for processing data as text, graphics, sound and moving images, is called a multimedia computer.

The computer equipment itself is called **hardware**. Most modern computers are multi processor systems, that is they have several processors which work co-operatively to handle specific tasks, for example managing screen graphics, complex arithmetical computations and handling peripherals. The main processing unit is called the central processing unit (CPU).

Peripherals can include additional memory, such as cache memory, which can greatly reduce processing time. Cache memory acts between the CPU and the main store. Disk cache holds data that has been read from a disk.

The following three types of disk drive are commonly used.

**Hard disk drives**, which use rigid magnetic disks enclosed in a sealed unit that cannot normally be removed from the computer.

**Floppy disk drives**, which, unlike hard drives, can be removed by the user.

**CD-ROM drives**, which use CD ROM disks, either as WORM drives (write once read many times) or as read-write disks.

Other input devices include mark sense readers, **optical mark readers** (OMR), **scanners**, **optical character recognition** scanners (OCR), **magnetic ink character recognition** devices (MICR) and **bar code readers**.

Output devices, sometimes known as display devices, include monochrome and colour monitors. Some monitors are multiscan or multisynch monitors, which enable the user to adjust the scan rates via a video adapter. Monitors on laptop and palmtop computers use liquid crystal displays (LCD). Other display devices include LEDs (light emitting diodes) and RGBs (red green blue).

A wide range of printers is available, including character printers, dot matrix printers, inkjet (sometimes called bubble jet) and laser printers. Impact printers, such as dot matrix and character printers, make a mark by striking an inked ribbon on the page. Inkjet printers use fine jets of quick drying ink directed onto the paper. Laser printers use electrostatics to attract toner onto a drum, which is transferred to the paper. Heat is then used to melt the toner onto the paper. Graphic plotters are an alternative output device that draws lines on paper by moving a pen electronically.

Computers can work individually as stand-alone computers, or can be linked together in networks. In a network a number of computers are linked together by wires, fibre optics, cables, microwave links or satellites in any combination to exchange information. Where the computers are relatively close to each other, for example in a school network, they are usually known as a LAN (local area network). Where they are geographically remote, they are known as a WAN – wide area network. Networking computers has the advantage not only of being an easy way to communicate between machines, but also of allowing them to share printers, large disk drives, CD ROMs and software.

Common networks include the following.

A **bus network**, is where each device is connected to the main communication line (called a bus).

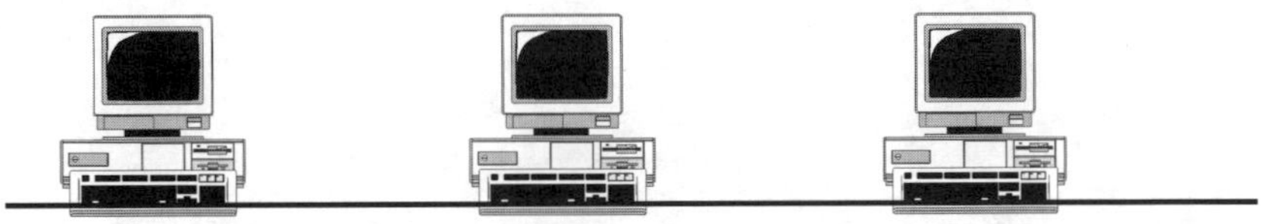

Sometimes this is done with spurs, as shown below.

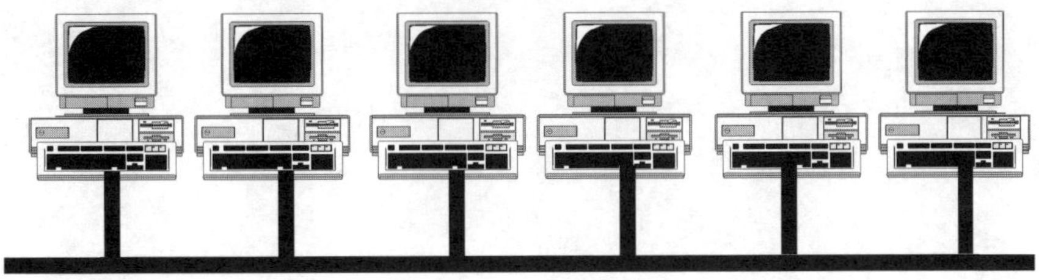

REVISION SUMMARY

A **ring network**, sometimes also called a loop, is where each of the devices is connected to a ring.

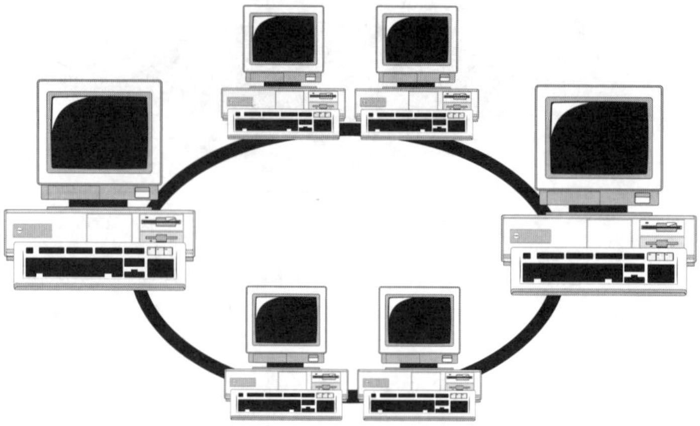

A **star network**, is where the main computer, sometimes called the hub, is at the centre and has separate connections to each computer.

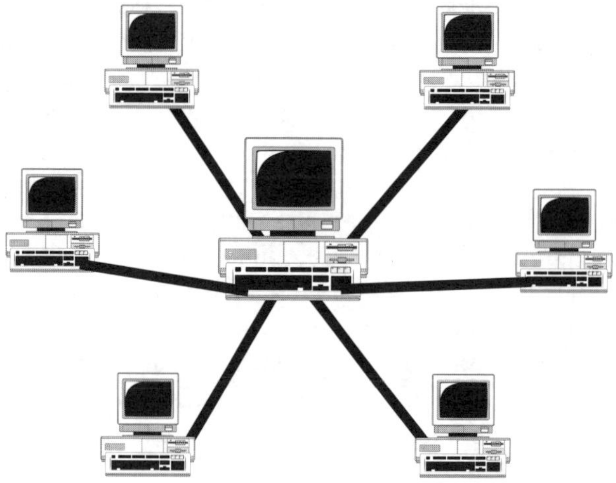

**If you need to revise this subject more thoroughly, see the relevant topics in the *Letts GCSE Information Technology Study Guide.***

QUESTIONS

**1** (a) The illustration below shows a computer and its peripherals.
Label the parts **A**, **B**, **C** and **D**.

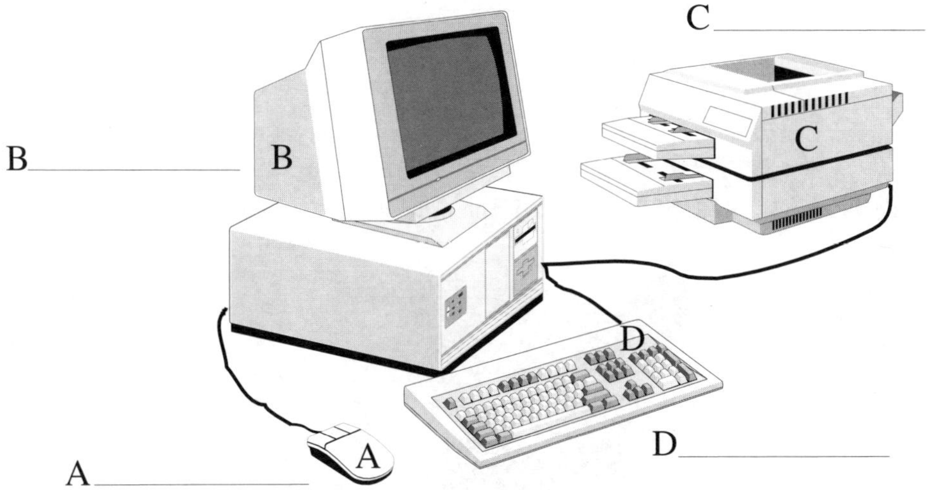


(4)

(b) For each part state if it is an input device or an output device.

A ...................................................................................................................

B ...................................................................................................................

C ...................................................................................................................

D ................................................................................................................... (4)

**2** The drawings below show three types of computer **input** device. Name each device.

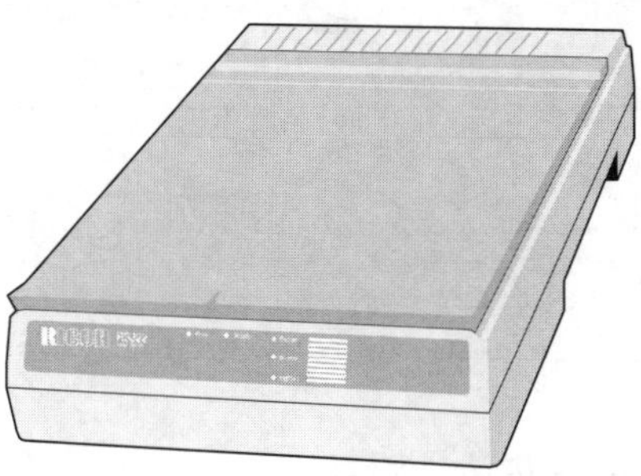

**A** ______________________

**B** ______________________

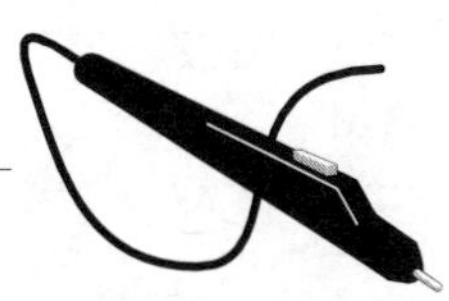

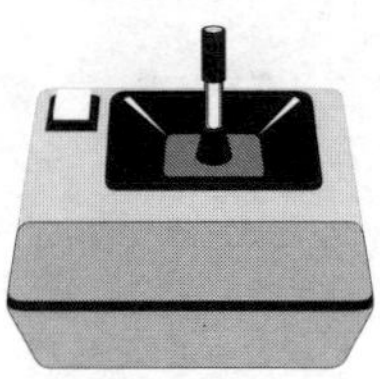

**C** ______________________

(3)

QUESTIONS

**3** In the spaces provided, state what the terms LAN and WAN stand for.

LAN ..........................................................................................................................

..........................................................................................................................

WAN ..........................................................................................................................

.......................................................................................................................... (2)

**4** In modern aircraft pilots 'fly by wire'. Explain what the term 'fly by wire' means.

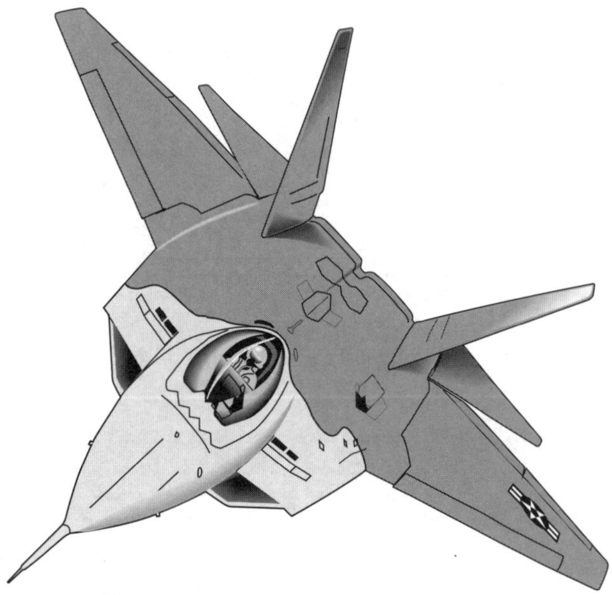

..........................................................................................................................

..........................................................................................................................

..........................................................................................................................

..........................................................................................................................

..........................................................................................................................

..........................................................................................................................

..........................................................................................................................

.......................................................................................................................... (6)

QUESTIONS

**5** (a) Information is stored in a computer. Name one storage medium which has a high data storage capacity that can be modified by the user.

........................................................................................................................ (1)

(b) Name one storage medium which has high capacity but cannot be changed by the user.

........................................................................................................................ (1)

(c) What does the term WORM stand for?

........................................................................................................................ (1)

(d) RAM and ROM are two types of computer memory.
Explain the difference between them and give one use of each.

........................................................................................................................

........................................................................................................................

........................................................................................................................

........................................................................................................................

........................................................................................................................ (4)

**6** Name the type of network shown in the picture below.

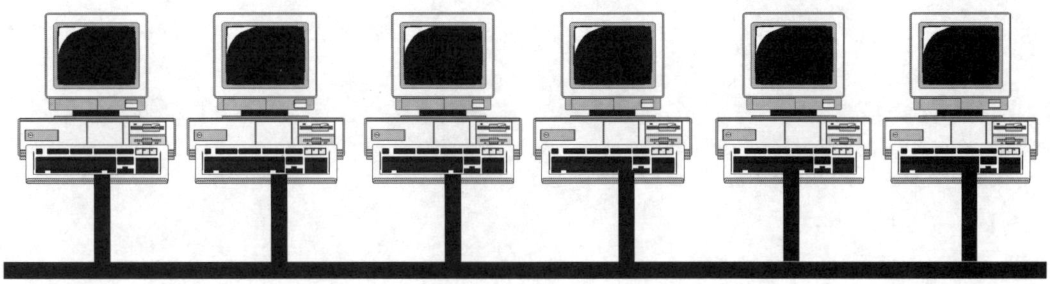

........................................................................................................................ (2)

QUESTIONS

7 Explain in detail how a computer-aided learning system could help a child to learn simple arithmetic.

........................................................................................................................................

........................................................................................................................................

........................................................................................................................................

........................................................................................................................................

........................................................................................................................................

........................................................................................................................................

........................................................................................................................................

........................................................................................................................................

........................................................................................................................................ (6)

REVISION SUMMARY

Word processing is the use of computing power to edit, format and produce typed letters and documents. By using a word processor, the operator is able to use stored text and a number of helpful facilities such as grammar checkers, spell checkers and mail merge.

Modern word processors also have document processing facilities. This allows for the integration of non-textual characters and the inclusion of diagrams, graphics, symbols and pictures.

Once you have opened a new document, it is advisable to save the document frequently. The first time you save a document you usually use a 'save as' command. Subsequently it is normal to use the 'save' command. The 'save' command overwrites the previous version of the document. The 'save as' command saves as a new document and you always need to give a new name when this command is used.

Word processors often include a 'cut and paste' command. This enables the operator to transfer blocks of text from one part of the document to another part, or even to another document.

Most word processors contain spell checkers. Spell checkers check the typed words against standard word lists stored in the software in the form of a dictionary. Dictionaries contain large numbers of pre-set words and specialist words can be added to customise the dictionary.

Word processors often contain a facility that allows for changes in both size and type of letter style, called fonts. They also allow for various types of type alignment called justification, including:

Fully justified text, where the text spacing is automatically adjusted to fill the page width, giving a straight line margin on both sides of the page.

Left alignment (justification), where the text starts at the left-hand margin, but appears uneven at the right-hand side.

Right alignment (justification), where text appears to be even at the right-hand margin, but uneven on the left-hand side.

Centred, where the text is evenly placed on either side of a centred margin.

As well as saving letters, it is common to save document templates in which the style, format and type are pre-set. A company may have its logo saved on the template to form its letterhead.

People often want to send similar letters to a large number of recipients, where the only difference is the name, address and perhaps minor variations in the body of the text. Standard letters can be saved so that they are always available for modification and saving as new documents to suit each particular letter required.

Mail merge utilises a file of clients' names, addresses and/or account details and allows these to be merged with a standard letter to produce individualised letters automatically. The file can be stored within the word processing software or can be linked to a database or spreadsheet application. One of the most common uses of mail merge is in the junk mail we receive through our letterboxes every day.

**If you need to revise this subject more thoroughly, see the relevant topics in the *Letts GCSE Information Technology Study Guide.***

QUESTIONS

1 Kearan and Xian often use a word processor to do their homework. Last week, they were both working at home on the computer when there was a power cut. Kearan lost all of his work, but Xian only lost part of his.

(a) What had Kearan forgotten to do?

..........................................................................................................................

.......................................................................................................................... (2)

(b) What is **AutoSave**?

..........................................................................................................................

.......................................................................................................................... (2)

(c) Describe when you would use '**save**' and when you would use '**save as**'.

..........................................................................................................................

..........................................................................................................................

..........................................................................................................................

..........................................................................................................................

.......................................................................................................................... (4)

(d) Kearan is waiting for his printer to print out 14 pages of text. After the third page, a message comes up on the screen to say **Printer Out Of Paper**.

(i) Where is the message '**Printer Out Of Paper**' stored?

..........................................................................................................................

.......................................................................................................................... (1)

(ii) Describe how the printer could have signalled to the computer that it needed more paper.

..........................................................................................................................

..........................................................................................................................

.......................................................................................................................... (2)

QUESTIONS

2 Four types of justification have been used below.
Label each illustration with the justification type used.

Dear Sir,

I wish to report a change of use for the main building of my house. As of the 13th of February, we intend to use the outbuilding for entertainment purposes.

A ..............................................

Dear Sir,

I wish to report a change of use for the main building of my house. As of the 13th of February, we intend to use the outbuilding for entertainment purposes.

B ..............................................

Dear Sir,

I wish to report a change of use for the main building of my house. As of the 13th of February, we intend to use the outbuilding for entertainment purposes.

C ..............................................

Dear Sir,

I wish to report a change of use for the main building of my house. As of the 13th of February, we intend to use the outbuilding for entertainment purposes.

D .............................................. (4)

3 A school office changes from manual typewriters to computerised word processors. Explain three ways in which word processing could help the school.

..............................................................................................................................

..............................................................................................................................

..............................................................................................................................

..............................................................................................................................

.............................................................................................................................. (6)

QUESTIONS

4 Describe what is meant by mail merge and state one example of its use.

..........................................................................................................................

..........................................................................................................................

..........................................................................................................................

..........................................................................................................................

.......................................................................................................................... (4)

5 Chloë often writes letters to her best friend using a word processor. Every time she carries out a spell check, it tells her that her friend's name is misspelt. She knows that it is spelt correctly.

(a) Describe how she can avoid this message appearing every time she spell checks her letters.

..........................................................................................................................

.......................................................................................................................... (1)

(b) Sometimes Chloë writes letters to magazines. She gets the same sort of message each time that the spell check looks at the postcodes. What action should Chloë take?

..........................................................................................................................

.......................................................................................................................... (1)

(c) Why could the action taken differ from the action taken for her best friend's name?

..........................................................................................................................

.......................................................................................................................... (1)

(d) It takes Chloë a long time to type in her best friend's address. How can Chloë make it easier to set up a page ready for a letter to her best friend?

..........................................................................................................................

..........................................................................................................................

.......................................................................................................................... (2)

**6** Two letters are shown below.

16 Springfield Close,
Warringfield,
Durham

19th July 1997

Dear <title> <surname>,

With reference to your account with us, number <account>, we regret to inform you that you appear not to have paid the amount of <amount> outstanding at the end of June.

Please pay this as soon as possible. If you have paid the amount in the last few days, please ignore this letter.

We look forward to hearing from you.

Yours sincerely

M. Counter
Accounts

---

16 Springfield Close,
Warringfield,
Durham

19th July 1997

Dear <title> <surname>,

With reference to your account with us, number <account>, we regret to inform you that you appear not to have paid the amount of <amount> outstanding at the end of June.

Please pay this as soon as possible. If you have paid the amount in the last few days, please ignore this letter.

We look forward to hearing from you.

Yours sincerely

M. Counter
Accounts

---

(a) State three changes that have been made to the second letter and for each change describe the word processing software feature that has been used.

Change 1: ..........................................................................................................

Feature used: .................................................................................................. (2)

Change 2: ..........................................................................................................

Feature used: .................................................................................................. (2)

Change 3: ..........................................................................................................

Feature used: .................................................................................................. (2)

(b) The letters use mail merge to add the name, address and account details. Underline the parts on the first letter that have been set up to use mail merge. (3)

QUESTIONS

7 Discuss the advantages and disadvantages of using word-processed text connected to electronic mail as opposed to a paper-based system.

Advantages: ..................................................................................................................

..................................................................................................................

..................................................................................................................

..................................................................................................................

Disadvantages: ..................................................................................................................

..................................................................................................................

..................................................................................................................

.................................................................................................................. (6)

It is hard to think of any situation where someone who stores large amounts of data would not be better off with it stored in a computer database. Any collection of related information could be called a database, even if a computer does not store the information.

A more traditional way of storing data was a card filing system. As files become larger finding the required information in a manual card system becomes more time consuming. Card records can become whole files of papers that take up a large amount of space. The other difficulty faced with a manual card system is deciding how the cards are to be indexed.

Computers can store a large amount of information in a small space. Although they can store large amounts of data, the information is still of no use unless it is linked together in some way and can be retrieved. Thus, a database is a collection of data linked together in a structured way. The terms used for this structure reflect the way a manual card filing system would be constructed.

| Name: | Kearan Cushing |
|---|---|
| Address: | The House |
| | 44 The Street |
| | Roman Town |
| Country: | England |
| Age: | 17 |

- Each card is a single record containing the data.
- The name, address, country and age are fields in the database.
- All of the cards together make up the records in the database file.
- Database software is supplied to the customer without files or data.

The first thing the user has to do is set up a data file in which collected data can be stored. This includes naming the file and sorting out the structure for each record. Each record will have a number of fields, which will require unique names.

| Field Name | Length | Type |
|---|---|---|
| Surname | 12 | Alpha-numeric |
| First name | 12 | Alpha-numeric |
| Date | 8 | Date |
| Age | 2 | Numeric |

In a manual system you would need to decide how the cards were going to be organised, for example are they going to be filed in alphabetical order by name? In practice, you would probably split the name into two sections, called first name and surname. This would help you sort the data alphabetically. In a computer-based system you can change the order when you ask for records to be displayed. Some computer-based systems do display records in card format, but most display the data in a grid format called a table (as shown above).

It is also common to state what type of data will be entered into each field, for example numbers, characters and date, and to state the length of each field. As shown above, you need more room for the address than you do for the age. The address contains both numeric data and characters. This is often called alpha-numeric data. The age is numeric data and would rarely be over two characters long. Other types of field include text, date and true/false.

REVISION SUMMARY

When you set up a database, you need to think carefully about the nature of the data you intend to enter.

| | | |
|---|---|---|
| Kearan Cushing | The House 44 The Street Roman Town | England 17 |
| Xian Cushing | The House 12 The Street Roman Town | England 15 |
| Zoë Downstreet | 12 Willow Road Real Place | England 12 |

In searching databases, the user needs to set up a search condition, often called a query, for example, a simple search would be surname = Cushing. You can search for single records or groups of records. Providing you have the correct data and the right fields you could carry out a much more complex search, for example, if you wanted all of the boys with birthdays on the 15th of February, you could select a search condition to find only the names with the right birthday and the correct sex.

The data you get when you have conducted a search is called a report. You can generate a large number of reports from a single database.

A report can be examined on the screen or printed out via a printer.

Reports can have added text, for example the dentist may send you a letter, which informs you of the need for a check-up. The letter will be generated as a report from the database showing the date of your last appointment, your name, your address and your patient number.

**Reminder of dental check-up**

Patient number:
Name:
Address:

Last appointment:

*Please note: You are due for a dental check-up. Please contact the office to arrange a suitable date and time.*

There are various types of databases, including the following.

- **Distributed databases** – used on networks of several computers, with each sharing part of the data and co-operating in making it available to the user.
- **Flat-file databases** – data is held in a single file, which allows only very simple structuring of data.
- **Hierarchical databases** – data is stored in a tree structure and can be accessed by users on a number of different levels. Data items are called nodes and the links are called branches.
- **Relational databases** – data is stored in a series of tables, each linked to each other by the database management system. This enables the user to view the data in a variety of ways and allows more flexibility in terms of data access and type of query.

**If you need to revise this subject more thoroughly, see the relevant topics in the *Letts GCSE Information Technology Study Guide.***

**1** Chloë is married with three children. She works as a secretary at a local hire company. She owns her own house and has a £40 000 mortgage from a building society. She enjoys reading and is a member of a mail order book club. She regularly uses a credit card to buy food from the supermarket.

(a) Based on this information about Chloë, write down four facts that could be stored in a computer database.

1 ..............................................................................................................................

2 ..............................................................................................................................

3 ..............................................................................................................................

4 .............................................................................................................................. (4)

(b) Explain the difference between information and data.

..............................................................................................................................

..............................................................................................................................

.............................................................................................................................. (2)

**2** There are a number of different types of databases.

(a) What is a distributed database?

..............................................................................................................................

..............................................................................................................................

..............................................................................................................................

.............................................................................................................................. (4)

(b) What is a relational database?

..............................................................................................................................

..............................................................................................................................

..............................................................................................................................

.............................................................................................................................. (4)

QUESTIONS

3 You are setting up a database for the school office. Look at the table below which shows the nature of the data collected, and state the type of field that you would use for each item of data.

| Field Name | Length | Field Type |
|---|---|---|
| Date | 8 | ........................................ |
| First Name | 12 | ........................................ |
| Surname | 12 | ........................................ |
| Boy-Girl | 1 | ........................................ |
| Age | 2 | ........................................ |
| Address | 18 | ........................................ |

(6)

4 In searching databases, the user needs to set up a search condition, often called a query. For example, if you want all of the boys with birthdays on the 15th of February, you can select a search condition to find only the names with the right birthday and the correct sex.

The table below shows one screen of a school database.

| Surname | Christian Name | Sex | Date (of Birth) | Address | Doctor |
|---|---|---|---|---|---|
| Asham | Mayer | M | 10-12-75 | 222 High Street | Smith |
| Cushing | Xian | M | 11-09-74 | 45 Main Road | Smith |
| Davidson | Jim | M | 15-02-76 | 21 The Slade | Johns |
| Inskip | David | M | 02-06-73 | 12 The Slade | Smith |
| Murray | Lesley | F | 23-06-74 | 6 Ash Row | Johns |
| Price | Jill | F | 29-09-73 | The Mill High Street | Smith |
| Yeomans | Barbara | F | 31-02-75 | 12 Flowerpot Road | Johns |

(a) State which field has been used to sort the data and how the data has been sorted.

........................................................................................................................ (1)

(b) There is a data entry error in the date field where one of the dates of birth has been incorrectly entered. State what it is.

........................................................................................................................ (1)

(c) Describe how the database could have been set up to avoid this data entry error.

........................................................................................................................ (1)

(d) Describe how you could search for all males born after 1994.

........................................................................................................................

........................................................................................................................

........................................................................................................................ (3)

(e) What is a field length?

........................................................................................................................ (1)

(f) What is a true/false field?

........................................................................................................................ (1)

**5** The owner of a security system shop uses a database for stock control.
Part of the stock control system is shown below.

| Reference | Description | Stock | Min Level | Order Quantity | Replace | Supplier Reference |
|---|---|---|---|---|---|---|
| 001 | Key | 11 | 10 | 20 | N | K003 |
| 002 | Lock | 10 | 15 | 20 | Y | K003 |
| 003 | Bell | 15 | 10 | 30 | N | B004 |
| 004 | Horn | 12 | 10 | 10 | N | B004 |
| 005 | Light | 8 | 12 | 50 | Y | B004 |
| 006 | Bell push | 15 | 20 | 50 | Y | K003 |

(a) What is a database Key field?

........................................................................................................................ (1)

(b) Which is the Key field in this database?

........................................................................................................................ (1)

(c) What is the reference of the stock items that need to be re-ordered?

........................................................................................................................ (1)

QUESTIONS

(d) Are they all to be ordered from the same supplier?

........................................................................................................................ (1)

(e) This database uses the following query language.

| **Field** | **Comparison** | **Value/Field** |
|---|---|---|

The search Description = Horn would find the item reference: 004.

(i) Write down the query that would find all items supplied by the supplier B004.

........................................................................................................................

........................................................................................................................

........................................................................................................................ (2)

(ii) Using logical operators to combine simple queries, write down the query which will show all of the items which need to be re-ordered as their stock levels are too low.

........................................................................................................................

........................................................................................................................

........................................................................................................................

........................................................................................................................

........................................................................................................................ (7)

**6** The school library uses a database system for recording the loan of books.

| Reference | Book | Out | On Loan to | Author |
|---|---|---|---|---|
| 001 | A Dog So Small | y | 103 | Philippa Pearce |
| 002 | The Sword in the Stone | y | 63 | TH White |
| 003 | Dragon Slayer | N | | Rosemary Sutcliffe |
| 004 | Alice in Wonderland | N | | Lewis Carroll |
| 005 | The Tale of Squirrel Nutkin | N | | Beatrix Potter |
| 006 | Burglar Bill | N | | Allan Ahlberg |

(a) Which is the unique field in this database?

.................................................................................................................................... (1)

(b) What type of field is the 'out' field?

.................................................................................................................................... (1)

(c) Describe the steps the school librarian must take to ensure the database is up-to-date and accurate.

....................................................................................................................................

....................................................................................................................................

....................................................................................................................................

.................................................................................................................................... (4)

(d) The school librarian wishes to generate automatic reminders when books are returned late. What other type of field would you add?

.................................................................................................................................... (1)

(e) Describe one advantage and one disadvantage of using a computer based system rather than a manual card system in the school library.

Advantage: ....................................................................................................................

....................................................................................................................................

Disadvantage: ................................................................................................................

.................................................................................................................................... (4)

# 4 Spreadsheets

REVISION SUMMARY

Information is data linked together. For example the information 'Steven is 16 years of age' contains two pieces of data: Steven (the name) and 16 years of age (some further information about Steven). A spreadsheet is a program into which you can enter both data and formulae. Spreadsheets can contain text, numeric data and pictures. The formulae in a spreadsheet can use all of the following signs, alongside other normal mathematical notation, for example bracket and exponentiation.

| | |
|---|---|
| + | to add |
| − | to subtract |
| / | for division |
| * | for multiplication |

Text can be used for labels and headings. Most spreadsheets can generate graphs.

Spreadsheets are a powerful use of the computer. They look something like a large sheet of squared paper on which you can enter your data and formulae. The computer can then perform calculations using the information given.

The rectangles on the 'paper' are usually called cells. The cells are divided into columns (marked by letters) and rows (marked by numbers). Thus, a column label refers to a vertical group of cells and a row label refers to a horizontal group of cells. A cell can contain letters or numbers and each cell has a unique reference called an address, for example H5 is column H, row 5.

| | A | B | C | D | E | F | G | H | I |
|---|---|---|---|---|---|---|---|---|---|
| 1 | | | | | | | | | |
| 2 | | | | | | | | | |
| 3 | | | | | | | | | |
| 4 | | | | | | | | | |
| 5 | | | | | | | | H5 | |
| 6 | | | | | | | | | |
| 7 | | | | | | | | | |
| 8 | | | | | | | | | |
| 9 | | | | | | | | | |

A range of formulae can be used in spreadsheets, and where these have been included in a cell, the spreadsheet will display the results of the calculation.

Spreadsheets also contain special types of formulae called functions. An example of a function is SUM(), used to calculate the sum or total of a row, column or block of cells.

| | A | B | C | D |
|---|---|---|---|---|
| 1 | | | | |
| 2 | | | | |
| 3 | | | | |
| 4 | | | Sum(C1:C3) | |

In the example, C4 would show the total of C1 + C2 + C3.

Most spreadsheets also allow you to produce charts and graphs. These could include pie charts, line charts, bar charts and scatter graphs. These charts can be displayed separately or included in a spreadsheet. Legends can be added.

Spreadsheets are often used for modelling. A computer model has to contain rules and data. The rules are important as they control the way the model works. The data can then be changed to predict an outcome. A simple model would be to produce a spreadsheet to show your pocket money and how much you spend on different things each week, for example on clothes and CDs. You could see how much surplus you had for savings if you reduced or increased spending on one or more of the items identified. A more complex model would be the country's balance of payments model. The government uses this model to set budget targets and see how well the country is doing.

There are two types of computer modelling, mathematical models and simulator models. The type of model used in a spreadsheet is a mathematical model. A flight simulator is another type of modelling. Both models have the advantage of allowing you to test out possibilities without danger. For example, the flight simulator can test the pilot's skills in an emergency situation before he or she flies the plane. The spreadsheet model can ask 'what if' questions of a nuclear reactor without danger to the public. The government's balance of payments model helps to predict what will happen if, for example, VAT rates go up, without affecting the financial markets.

If you were on a diet, you could set up a computer model to map the calorific intake during the day. You could then experiment with different menus and see which gave the best value and balance. This would avoid trial and error.

Before setting up a spreadsheet therefore, you need to consider what questions you want to ask and what output you need to achieve. You can then work out the rules for the model and create the necessary formula.

Spreadsheets can link with other software applications. Dynamic data exchange is one method of simultaneously exchanging data between two or more applications. Most of today's software contains special paste facilities, whereby links can easily be made, between spreadsheets and between a spreadsheet and another software package.

Object linking and embedding (OLE) is an important way in which today's software creates dynamic links between two documents. In object embedding, the embedded object from the source document is placed physically into the destination document, so that the resulting file contains the information needed by both documents.

**If you need to revise this subject more thoroughly, see the relevant topics in the *Letts GCSE Information Technology Study Guide.***

1 The school office uses a spreadsheet to keep track of textbook sales.

| | A | B | C | D |
|---|---|---|---|---|
| 1 | *Description* | *Selling price (£)* | *Number sold* | *Sales value* |
| 2 | ICT Textbook | 11.75 | 104 | 1222.00 |
| 3 | Food Textbook | 12.50 | 94 | 1175.00 |
| 4 | Maths Textbook | 14.00 | 180 | 2520.00 |
| 5 | English Textbook | 10.75 | 190 | 2042.50 |
| 6 | Science Textbook | 16.50 | 130 | 2145.00 |
| 7 | **Total sales** | | **698** | **9104.50** |
| 8 | | | | |

(a) Write down the formulae that would be entered for each of the shaded cells.

| | A | B | C | D |
|---|---|---|---|---|
| 1 | *Description* | *Selling price (£)* | *Number sold* | *Sales value* |
| 2 | ICT Textbook | 11.75 | 104 | 1222.00 |
| 3 | Food Textbook | 12.50 | 94 | 1175.00 |
| 4 | Maths Textbook | 14.00 | 180 | 2520.00 |
| 5 | English Textbook | 10.75 | 190 | |
| 6 | Science Textbook | 16.50 | 130 | 2145.00 |
| 7 | **Total sales** | | | |
| 8 | | | | |

...............................................................................................................................

............................................................................................................................... (4)

(b) Write down two advantages to the school in using formulae in a spreadsheet.

Advantage 1: ...............................................................................................

...............................................................................................................................

Advantage 2: ...............................................................................................

............................................................................................................................... (4)

(c) The school decides to improve the spreadsheet by adding the cost price of each book and setting up the spreadsheet to calculate the profits from sales.
The modified spreadsheet is shown below.

| | A | B | C | D | E | F |
|---|---|---|---|---|---|---|
| 1 | *Description* | *Selling price (£)* | *Number sold* | *Sales value* | *Purchase price* | *Profit on sales* |
| 2 | ICT Textbook | 11.75 | 104 | 1222.00 | 10.00 | 182.00 |
| 3 | Food Textbook | 12.50 | 94 | 1175.00 | 10.25 | 211.50 |
| 4 | Maths Textbook | 14.00 | 180 | 2520.00 | 12.50 | 270.00 |
| 5 | English Textbook | 10.75 | 190 | 2042.50 | 9.25 | 285.00 |
| 6 | Science Textbook | 16.50 | 130 | 2145.00 | 14.00 | 325.00 |
| 7 | **Total sales** | | **698** | **9104.50** | | **1273.50** |
| 8 | | | | | | |

Show the formula that could have been used in the shaded cell.

| | A | B | C | D | E | F |
|---|---|---|---|---|---|---|
| 1 | *Description* | *Selling price (£)* | *Number sold* | *Sales value* | *Purchase price* | *Profit on sales* |
| 2 | ICT Textbook | 11.75 | 104 | 1222.00 | 10.00 | 182.00 |
| 3 | Food Textbook | 12.5 | 94 | 1175.00 | 10.25 | 211.50 |
| 4 | Maths Textbook | 14 | 180 | 2520.00 | 12.50 | 270.00 |
| 5 | English Textbook | 10.75 | 190 | 2042.50 | 9.25 | |
| 6 | Science Textbook | 16.5 | 130 | 2145.00 | 14.00 | 325.00 |
| 7 | **Total sales** | | **698** | **9104.50** | | **988.50** |
| 8 | | | | | | |

.............................................................................................................................. (2)

(d) The profit shown in F7 is to be included on another spreadsheet, which shows the school's financial position. The data is to be updated automatically. Describe how this could be achieved.

..............................................................................................................................

..............................................................................................................................

.............................................................................................................................. (4)

**2** A local hotel uses a spreadsheet to model restaurant profit margins.
To calculate the column headed 'Hours', the restaurant has divided the total number of one item made by the overall time taken by the chef to make a batch of that item. The ingredient costs have been calculated by dividing the total purchase price of the amounts of ingredients used by the number of items produced. Two chefs are used. The pastry chef is paid at a higher rate per hour than the general chef.

| | A | B | C | D | E | F | G |
|---|---|---|---|---|---|---|---|
| 1 | **Menu Costing Sheet** | | | | | | |
| | | | | | | | |
| 2 | **Lunch Time Set Menu** | | | | | | |
| 3 | *Description* | *Hours* | *Labour Cost/hour (£)* | *Ingredient Cost (£)* | *Overheads (£)* | *Cost (£)* | |
| 4 | Vegetable Soup | 0.25 | 5.60 | 0.50 | 0.20 | | |
| 5 | Salad | 0.30 | 5.60 | 1.50 | 0.10 | | |
| 6 | Bread roll | 0.10 | 6.50 | 0.10 | 0.12 | | |
| 7 | Butter | 0.00 | 0.00 | 0.08 | 0.11 | | |
| 8 | Apple Pie | 0.30 | 6.50 | 1.25 | 0.30 | | |
| 9 | | | | | | | |
| 10 | | | | | | | |

(a) Write in the formula that would be entered into F4 to calculate the total cost of the vegetable soup menu item.

Formula: ........................................................................................................... (2)

QUESTIONS

(b) How would you set up the formula in the other cells under column F?

Method: ..............................................................................................................

.............................................................................................................................. (2)

(c) What formula would the restaurant use to calculate the total cost of the meal?

Formula: ............................................................................................................ (2)

(d) The pastry chef has asked for a pay rise of £0.20 per hour. The restaurant does not wish to put up its prices. It presently works on a very low profit margin.
Explain fully how the computer model can help the restaurant to explore changes in profit margins and explore ways of maintaining a profit whilst increasing the pay of the pastry chef.

..............................................................................................................................

..............................................................................................................................

..............................................................................................................................

..............................................................................................................................

..............................................................................................................................

..............................................................................................................................

..............................................................................................................................

.............................................................................................................................. (8)

**3** A local dairy intends to set up a milk round. The dairy produces a range of products including:
Full cream milk @ 45p per pint
Semi-skimmed milk @ 43p per pint
Skimmed milk @ 42p per pint
Double cream @ £1.00 per pint
Single cream @ 85p per pint
Each product is sold in pint and two pint containers. Two pint containers are double the cost of single containers less a 10p discount.
The dairy intends to use a spreadsheet to manage the ordering and invoicing of customers in the village.

(a) List two other pieces of information the dairy needs before it can set up the spreadsheet.

Information 1: ................................................................................................. (1)

Information 2: ................................................................................................. (1)

(b) In the spaces provided show the main elements of the spreadsheet. (6)

| | | | | | | |
|---|---|---|---|---|---|---|
| | | | | | | |
| | | | | | | |
| | | | | | | |
| | | | | | | |

(c) Describe how the dairy could use your spreadsheet to produce a weekly invoice for the customer.

.......................................................................................................................

.......................................................................................................................

....................................................................................................................... (3)

(d) Show what formula would be used to help the dairy send invoices to its customers.

.......................................................................................................................

....................................................................................................................... (4)

**4** Your youth club is running a skiing holiday to Italy. You have been asked to set up a spreadsheet to show the various costs of transport and hotels.
Describe the main features of a spreadsheet that will allow the data to be analysed to find the best possible prices for hotel bookings and transport.

.......................................................................................................................

.......................................................................................................................

.......................................................................................................................

.......................................................................................................................

.......................................................................................................................

....................................................................................................................... (6)

QUESTIONS

5 Your school has decided to introduce a computerised system for checking the attendance of pupils. The system will use SMART cards issued to pupils and they will scan their cards through a reader on arriving at school. Describe the main stages that need to be undertaken before the system is operational.

..........................................................................................................................

..........................................................................................................................

..........................................................................................................................

..........................................................................................................................

..........................................................................................................................

.......................................................................................................................... (5)

Data logging is the automatic recording of data for later use. Where a computer is used, sensors usually collect the data via an interface box. A computer program is designed to receive signals from the interface box and the data is then stored in the computer. Many modern interface boxes have the ability to store data themselves. Data can then be analysed later.

In order that the data logging system can work, it requires sensors. Sensors include analogue and digital sensors and can be passive or active devices. The most common sensors are analogue. A sensor simply measures some physical quantity such as pressure, rate of flow, humidity or proximity, and turns this into analogue or digital electrical outputs. Where the sensor requires no external electrical source, it is called a passive device. Where it requires external voltage, it is called an active device.

Sensors can be used to register data in a data logging system remotely from the computer. The data logging interface box can be pre-programmed to work in a remote situation, for example to record pH levels in a local pond. Sensors can be used to collect all sorts of data, including temperature, heartbeat, speed, chemical change, movements and light levels.

It is common to use a data logging system where it would be dangerous or difficult to take manual recordings, for example in a nuclear reactor. Data logging systems can be programmed to take recordings at any required interval, for example every second, every fortnight or every 10 years.

Before being used, data logging equipment needs to be calibrated.

Once data has been captured, it can be used in a number of ways. Before it can be used, it must be processed either into a form that humans can understand, for example, charts, lists or pictorial images, or into a computer language as part of a control device.

## Control devices

Often, the data is used as an input to a computerised control device, for example a house central heating system which, having collected data from the thermostat, processes the data and automatically lights the boiler and switches on a pump to circulate hot water to either the hot water cylinder or radiators.

Other household control devices include temperature controls on ovens, safety cutouts in microwaves and cookers, water temperature sensors in washing machines and dishwashers, sprinkler devices and burglar alarms.

All control device systems have to have an input, for example the data collected by the sensor. They must also have a process, either in the interface box or the computer system where, for example, the analogue signal could be converted to a digital signal or processed in a pre-programmed way. Finally, they have an output (for example a display of the data on a screen or as a printout or a sound) or control of another device (for example a motor).

A system is usually designed as a flowchart, although block diagrams and logic diagrams are also used. What is important is that precise details are given for each stage of the system, and that the diagram clearly shows where any links occur, for example feedback loops.

- **Common input devices**: switches (push/tilt/reed/microswitch), light-dependent resistor, thermistor (heat sensor), light pen and infrared beams.
- **Common output devices**: bulbs, light-emitting diodes, buzzers, loudspeakers, motors, valves and bells.
- **Processing software**: there are many different pieces of software written to control output devices in response to signals from sensors. The most common program used in schools is *Logo*. *Logo* can be used to control a screen image or drive an output device, such as a floor turtle.

**If you need to revise this subject more thoroughly, see the relevant topics in the** ***Letts GCSE Information Technology Study Guide.***

QUESTIONS

1 The following instructions can be used to control a floor turtle.

| | |
|---|---|
| Forward *N* | move *N* centimetres forward |
| Backward *N* | move *N* centimetres backward |
| Turn left *T* | turn left *T* degrees |
| Turn right *T* | turn right *T* degrees |
| Pen down | place the pen on the paper |
| Pen up | lift the pen off the paper |

Write a set of instructions to make the turtle draw a square with sides of 50 cm.

..........

..........

..........

..........

.......... (5)

2 Write down **two** control devices, which could be used in a cooker.

Device 1: ..........

Device 2: .......... (2)

3 The meteorological office collects its weather data using data logging equipment. Specify one other situation in which you would use a data logging device.

.......... (1)

4 Modern factories often use robotic equipment to transport goods around the factory. These robots follow white lines painted on the floor. Name one sensor which could be used to prevent the robot from bumping into somebody.

..........

..........

.......... (3)

QUESTIONS

5 Describe three ways in which Information Technology equipment could be used in a scientific research laboratory.

........................................................................................................................

........................................................................................................................

........................................................................................................................ (3)

6 Ring two applications which use control systems.

| | |
|---|---|
| **Central heating** | **Database** |
| **Word processor** | **Traffic lights** (2) |

7 An information system is used to count the number of cars entering and leaving a car park. It uses two infrared beams to do this.

(a) Explain how the information system can count the number of cars going into or leaving the car park using the two beams.

........................................................................................................................

........................................................................................................................

........................................................................................................................ (2)

(b) The car park attendant needs to test the information system to make sure it works correctly. Describe two tests that he could make.

........................................................................................................................

........................................................................................................................

........................................................................................................................ (2)

(c) The car park attendant has checked the system and is satisfied that it works correctly. However, a number of people complain that, having entered the car park, there is no parking space. Describe two limitations of the design of this information system that could allow this to happen, and how these limitations could be corrected.

Limitation 1: ..........................................................................................

........................................................................................................................

Correction 1: ..........................................................................................

........................................................................................................................

Letts Q&A

Limitation 2: ....................................................................................................

....................................................................................................

Correction 2: ....................................................................................................

.................................................................................................... (4)

# Desktop publishing

REVISION SUMMARY

Desktop publishing allows you to organise text and pictures in documents such as posters, leaflets, books, newspapers and packaging.

Most desktop publishing packages provide basic text entry and editing facilities, basic drawing facilities and the ability to import files from other drawing and word-processing programs, or pictures scanned into the computer using a scanner or digital camera. A number of packages provide collections of ready-made pictures called Clip-art.

Most desktop publishing programs allow you to set up a page, including setting margins, orientation of the page, for example portrait or landscape, and the location of graphics and text. Another advantage of desktop publishing packages is the ability to change the lettering style, called fonts or typeface. The size of fonts is measured in points that actually relate to the old Imperial inch measurement. The larger the point size, the larger the lettering. 72 point is the largest that you are likely to use for a headline in a newspaper. Alongside alignment, tabs and hyphenation, most desktop publishing packages also allow for changes in kerning. This refers to changes in space between characters.

Most desktop publishing programs allow you to rearrange and alter blocks of text on the page, even when you have completed your initial layout. Pictures and text blocks can be dragged into new positions. Some desktop publishing programs allow you to 'flow' text around graphics, or from one column or one page to another.

Invisible or visible grids can be created and most programs show rulers along the top and left-hand side of the screen, to help with positioning.

The main advantage of using a desktop publishing package is that is allows the integration of text and graphics. Pictures, maps, graphs and diagrams not only portray information more clearly, but also break up a page and make a document look more inviting. Pictures can be stored in a number of different formats for use in desktop publishing packages. The most common formats are TIF, GIF, EPS, PIC, PCX and BMP.

Desktop publishing packages often allow for changes in the resolution of documents. Resolution is measured in dots per inch (dpi). The higher the dpi, the better the quality of the image. Most modern laser printers print at 600 dpi.

**If you need to revise this subject more thoroughly, see the relevant topics in the *Letts GCSE Information Technology Study Guide.***

QUESTIONS

1 The text for magazines is often initially produced on a word processor. Writers often work from homes situated across the country and sometimes abroad. Where more than one writer is working on an article, the text needs to be transferred electronically between the two writers. A viewdata system could be used.

(a) Describe the steps needed to transfer the article electronically.

..........................................................................................................................................

.......................................................................................................................................... (2)

(b) Describe how you could use a desktop publishing package to convert the article into a magazine article incorporating pictures as well as text.

..........................................................................................................................................

..........................................................................................................................................

..........................................................................................................................................

.......................................................................................................................................... (4)

2 Simple drawing tools are provided with most desktop publishing packages. Six different types of drawing tool are listed below. For each drawing tool, state its use.

(a) Pre-set shapes tool.

Use: ..................................................................................................................................

(b) Fill command.

Use: ..................................................................................................................................

(c) Colour palette.

Use: ..................................................................................................................................

(d) Text tool.

Use: ..................................................................................................................................

(e) Freehand drawing tool.

Use: ..................................................................................................................................

(f) Rotation tool.

Use: .................................................................................................................................. (6)

**3** Compare a range of methods of obtaining pictures or graphics for inclusion in a desktop published package.

..........................................................................................................................

..........................................................................................................................

..........................................................................................................................

..........................................................................................................................

..........................................................................................................................

..........................................................................................................................

..........................................................................................................................

..........................................................................................................................

..........................................................................................................................

.......................................................................................................................... (8)

# 7 Information systems in society

**REVISION SUMMARY**

It is hard to think of many companies or service providers who do not make use of IT. Even in our homes, we are surrounded by control systems and microchip units in our washing machines, central heating systems, watches, clocks and telephone systems. All rely upon IT. Daily we receive advertising literature through the post that has been mailed as a direct result of data files, which contain our personal data.

Computer systems contain a large amount of valuable personal data. Protecting this data is important both to the individual to whom the data relates and to the person holding the data. Incorrect data can result not only in a loss of income for the end user, but also in a negative outcome for the original person. There are a number of regulations designed to protect people from the misuse of data. The Data Protection Act 1984 sets out requirements that control the use of personal data stored in computer systems. It requires data users to ensure the accuracy and appropriateness of data. It gives individuals the right to see data stored on them. End users have to provide information about the nature, purpose and range of data that they hold, and sign a public register.

They must collect data in a fair way, and can only use the data for the purpose they specify in the register. Data must be collected and updated and should be destroyed once it has been used for the purpose specified. Companies can sell data without referring to the person(s) concerned, but only if they have stated in the register that they wish to do this. Word-processed documents are completely exempt from the Data Protection Act, as is any data where individuals cannot be identified.

Examples of data that is held legally on individuals, and is often freely available, include:

- postal addresses and post codes;
- Council Tax valuations;
- the electoral roll;
- telephone directories.

A large number of companies hold data on individuals and, as they have registered under the Data Protection Act, it is perfectly legal for them to do so. This data is often sold as lists to companies wishing to use it for telesales or 'junk' mailings.

The Computer Misuse Act 1990 aimed to prevent 'hacking' and introduced three new offences related to unauthorised computer access, modification and deletion of data.

To prevent hacking, companies registered under the Data Protection Act have to build safeguards into their systems. These safeguards include passwords and other types of personal identification systems. When transmitting important data, they often use encryption systems that make the data useless to anyone who does not have the correct decoding logarithm. Rooms containing sensitive data have to be kept locked and protected.

Information systems can be found in shops, controlling sales, stock levels, re-ordering and producing our receipts. In factories they control stock, parts ordering and workflow. In the streets they control lighting, traffic flow and communications networks, such as mobile telephones and pagers. In transportation they are used to control aircraft and train movements. Modern motor vehicles are collections of complex control systems. In our hospitals there are a large number of computer-controlled systems.

Examiners like to set questions in a real context and some examination papers are set around a particular context, for example, a motorway service station.

**If you need to revise this subject more thoroughly, see the relevant topics in the *Letts GCSE Information Technology Study Guide.***

1 A company called Alpha gains data by carrying out a street survey. Its database contains names, addresses, family details, socio-economic groupings and buying habits. It registers this information under the Data Protection Act.

(a) Is the company acting in accordance with the law?

.............................................................................................................................. (1)

(b) A telesales company called Beta requires data on buying habits. It offers to purchase data from Alpha. Under what circumstances would it be legal for Alpha to sell the data to Beta?

..............................................................................................................................

..............................................................................................................................

..............................................................................................................................

.............................................................................................................................. (2)

2 A doctor's surgery changes from a manual record-keeping system to a computerised system. The surgery records will contain personal information of a confidential nature.

(a) Name **three** items of personal data that the surgery could hold about you. (*Other than name and address.*)

Data 1: ..............................................................................................................

Data 2: ..............................................................................................................

Data 3: .............................................................................................................. (3)

(b) How could the surgery protect and secure the data?

..............................................................................................................................

..............................................................................................................................

..............................................................................................................................

.............................................................................................................................. (2)

(c) Would the surgery need to register under the Data Protection Act?

.............................................................................................................................. (1)

QUESTIONS

3 A high street bank stores large amounts of information on computer files.
Discuss the possible consequences for you, as a customer, of inaccurate data being held in the bank's computer system.

..........................................................................................................

..........................................................................................................

..........................................................................................................

.......................................................................................................... (4)

4 The Police use a computer database to help them in their work of detecting and preventing crime.

(a) Name two ways in which the Police might use computer-stored data to prevent crime.

Way 1: ..........................................................................................................

..........................................................................................................

Way 2: ..........................................................................................................

.......................................................................................................... (2)

(b) Name two ways in which the Police might use computer-stored data to solve crimes.

Way 1: ..........................................................................................................

..........................................................................................................

Way 2: ..........................................................................................................

.......................................................................................................... (2)

5 When you purchase goods from a supermarket, a point of sale (POS) system captures the data.

(a) How is the data captured by the system?

.......................................................................................................... (2)

(b) Where is the price of the item held in the system?

.......................................................................................................... (2)

(c) Give two advantages to you as a customer of having a POS system.

Advantage 1: ..........................................................................................................

..........................................................................................................................

Advantage 2: ..........................................................................................................

.......................................................................................................................... (4)

(d) Give two advantages to the manager of the supermarket.

Advantage 1: ..........................................................................................................

..........................................................................................................................

Advantage 2: ..........................................................................................................

.......................................................................................................................... (4)

**6** Whenever you give your name and address to a shop assistant, there is a likelihood that it will be held on a computer database. The Data Protection Act is there to protect you from misuse of this data.

(a) Give three rules that a shop must obey.

Rule 1: ..........................................................................................................

Rule 2: ..........................................................................................................

Rule 3: .......................................................................................................... (3)

(b) Give three examples of data which need not be registered under the Act.

Data 1: ..........................................................................................................

Data 2: ..........................................................................................................

Data 3: .......................................................................................................... (3)

**7** The Internet is a worldwide network containing huge amounts of data.

(a) Give **two** ways that the Internet might be useful to a researcher working at home.

Way 1: ..........................................................................................................

Way 2: .......................................................................................................... (4)

QUESTIONS

(b) A number of governments wish to place controls on the type of information available on the Internet.

(i) Explain why governments would want to control information on the Internet.

..........................................................................................................................

..........................................................................................................................

..........................................................................................................................

.......................................................................................................................... (4)

(ii) Explain why such control might be opposed.

..........................................................................................................................

..........................................................................................................................

..........................................................................................................................

.......................................................................................................................... (4)

**8** A large number of shops now use bar code systems. Each item is given a unique reference number, for example a tin of beans in a supermarket could be give a unique reference number of YBCD1998.

(a) Give two reasons why bar codes are used.

Reason 1: ..........................................................................................................

Reason 2: .......................................................................................................... (2)

(b) State the name of two data items that are often used in bar codes.

Data Item 1: ......................................................................................................

Data Item 2: ...................................................................................................... (2)

(c) Sometimes the bar code reader fails to read the code properly.

(i) State how the checkout operator knows that the bar code has not been read properly.

..........................................................................................................................

.......................................................................................................................... (1)

(ii) What must the checkout operator do when the bar code will not read properly?

..........................................................................................................................

.......................................................................................................................... (1)

**9** When you use your own disks in a networked system, the network manager has to be careful to ensure that you do not transfer a computer virus.

(a) What is a 'computer virus'?

..........................................................................................................................

.......................................................................................................................... (2)

(b) State two precautions that the network manager could take to prevent the transfer of a virus.

Precaution 1: ..........................................................................................................

Precaution 2: .......................................................................................................... (2)

# 8 Mock examination paper

QUESTIONS

*Try to complete this paper in one sitting of* ***one and a half hours****.*

**1** A chain of dentists is about to open a new surgery in your area. The chain, called *Teeth*, has a head office 20 miles away. They use computerised systems in almost all aspects of their work. This will be the sixth surgery in the chain. All of the surgeries are about 6 miles apart.

(a) The new receptionist will use a computer system with a touch pad, monitor, keyboard, laser printer and video camera. Fill in the chart below stating whether the device is an input or output device. (5)

| Device | Type of device input/output |
|---|---|
| touch pad | |
| monitor | |
| keyboard | |
| laser printer | |
| video camera | |

(b) All of the computers at the surgery are networked. List three advantages of networking.

Advantage 1 ..................................................................................................................

Advantage 2 ..................................................................................................................

Advantage 3 .................................................................................................................. (3)

(c) The computers at the dentist are linked together by a fibre optic LAN network. What do the letters LAN stand for?

L..................................................................

A ..................................................................

N .................................................................. (1)

(d) The chain of dentists has decided to link their individual networks together so that each dentist surgery can link with the others over the six miles separating them. What type of network is this?

.................................................................................................................................... (1)

Letts Q&A

2 The dentist notifies all of its patients of when they are due for a check-up. The computer system does this automatically by linking the main database with the word processor. Part of the database is shown below.

| Last Name | First Name | Address | Post Code | Last Apt | DoB | Dentist |
|---|---|---|---|---|---|---|
| Cushing | Cerri | 22 Mill Street, Old Town | GG2 DD3 | 5 June 99 | 15-02-1952 | D Smith |
| Cushing | Xian | 22 Mill Street, Old Town | GG2 DD3 | 5 June 99 | 12-06-1965 | D Smith |
| Inskip | Avon | 34 The Rowans, Glades | GG2 DE4 | 5 July 98 | 01-07-1968 | M Jones |
| Inskip | Chloe | 34 The Rowans, Glades | GG2 DE4 | 5 July 99 | 14-05-1991 | M Jones |
| Yeomans | Barbara | Sewing Shop, High Street | GG2 DS3 | 18 May 98 | 03-09-1972 | D Smith |
| Yeomans | David | Sewing Shop, High Street | GG2 DS3 | 18 January 99 | 02-11-1876 | D Smith |
| Yeomans | Geoffrey | Sewing Shop, High Street | GG2 DS3 | 18 May 98 | 08-08-1956 | D Smith |

(a) (i) What fields have been used to sort the database?

Primary Field ..........................................................................................................

Secondary Field .......................................................................................... (2)

(ii) The receptionist has clearly made a data entry error in one of the fields. What is the data entry error and which field is it in?

Error and field ........................................................................................... (2)

(iii) For each field, state the type of field that could be used to set up the database. (4)

| Field | Type of Field |
|---|---|
| Last Name | |
| Address | |
| Post Code | |
| DoB | |

(iv) What is a true/false field?

.................................................................................................................. (1)

(v) What is meant by field length?

.................................................................................................................. (1)

QUESTIONS

(vi) It is now September 1999. Write a search to find all of the people who need a dental appointment soon because their last visit was over 6 months ago.

..........................................................................................................................

..........................................................................................................................

..........................................................................................................................

.......................................................................................................................... (2)

(b) An outline of a mail-merged reminder letter is shown below.

> Cerri Cushing
> 22 Mill Street,
> Old Town
> GG2 DD3
>
> Dear Cerri
>
> You are due for a dental check-up. Please contact our office on 01432 888888 to make an appropriate appointment.
>
> Yours sincerely
>
> D Smith

In the space below add the missing fields used in the mail merged letter. ...............(4)

<First Name>
<Address>

Dear

You are due for a dental check-up. Please contact our office on 01432 888888 to make an appropriate appointment.

Yours sincerely

(c) (i) The dentist will have confidential information on its patients held on computer. What is the name of the Act which protects them from misuse of this data?

Name of Act .................................................................................................... (2)

(ii) State three requirements of the act.

Requirement 1 ....................................................................................................

....................................................................................................

Requirement 2 ....................................................................................................

....................................................................................................

Requirement 3 ....................................................................................................

.................................................................................................... (3)

(iii) State two steps that could be taken to prevent unauthorised users from accessing the information stored on the computer system.

Step 1 ....................................................................................................

....................................................................................................

Step 2 ....................................................................................................

.................................................................................................... (2)

**3** All of the ordering of stock and the invoicing of dental treatment is done on the computer. Part of the dentist's spreadsheet is shown below.

| | A | B | C | D | E | F | G |
|---|---|---|---|---|---|---|---|
| 1 | *Stock Description* | *Reference* | *Quantity* | *Unit* | *Unit Price (£)* | *Stock Value (£)* | |
| 2 | Amalgam | AB306 | 100mg | 10mg | 8.64 | 86.4 | |
| 3 | Mouthwash | AB604 | 2ltr | 1ltr | 2.22 | 4.44 | |
| 4 | UL5 Retainer Pin | UL456 | 34 | 10 | 3.98 | | |
| 5 | Composite Filling | MK304 | 500mg | 100 mg | 5.66 | | |
| 6 | | | | | | | |
| 7 | Total Stock Value | | | | | | |

In column B the dentist has included a unique reference number. The first two letters refer to the supplier of the stock items.

(a) What is the formula that should be used in cell F4?

Formula .................................................................................................... (1)

QUESTIONS

(b) What formula should be used in cell F7?

Formula .................................................................................................................. (2)

(c) Why would the dentist want to have a unique reference number for each stock item?

Reason ...................................................................................................................

..............................................................................................................................

..............................................................................................................................

.............................................................................................................................. (4)

**4** (a) What is the main difference between an intranet and the internet?

..............................................................................................................................

..............................................................................................................................

..............................................................................................................................

..............................................................................................................................

.............................................................................................................................. (4)

(b) Describe how the internet could be used to help promote the dental practice.

..............................................................................................................................

..............................................................................................................................

..............................................................................................................................

.............................................................................................................................. (2)

(c) Describe at least three ways in which the internet could be of help to the dentists working in the practice.

..............................................................................................................................

..............................................................................................................................

..............................................................................................................................

..............................................................................................................................

..............................................................................................................................

..............................................................................................................................

.............................................................................................................................. (6)

(d) (i) Describe one advantage and one disadvantage of using e-mail over conventional post.

..............................................................................................................................

..............................................................................................................................

..............................................................................................................................

..............................................................................................................................

..............................................................................................................................

.............................................................................................................................. (4)

(ii) State one advantage and one disadvantage in using e-mail over conventional telephones.

..............................................................................................................................

..............................................................................................................................

..............................................................................................................................

..............................................................................................................................

..............................................................................................................................

.............................................................................................................................. (4)

# Answers

## 1 COMPUTERS AND PERIPHERALS

| Question | | Answer | Mark |
|---|---|---|---|
| 1 | (a) | A Mouse | 1 |
| | | B Monitor or VDU | 1 |
| | | C Printer (Laser Printer) | 1 |
| | | D Keyboard | 1 |
| | (b) | A Input | 1 |
| | | B Output | 1 |
| | | C Output | 1 |
| | | D Input | 1 |

**Examiner's tip** Look carefully at the drawings before you answer. It is easy to gain marks on this type of question, but you must give the correct technical name, for example no marks would be awarded in A for TV or Screen. The correct name is Monitor or VDU. Remember also that anything that puts information into the computer is an INPUT device, anything that displays information out of the computer is an OUTPUT device.

| Question | | Answer | Mark |
|---|---|---|---|
| 2 | | A Scanner | 1 |
| | | B Stylus or Light Pen | 1 |
| | | C Joystick | 1 |

**Examiner's tip** A clue is given in the question, as you know they are all input devices. If you are not quite sure what one of the drawings represents, guess an answer – remembering that they are all computer input devices. To help you examiners often highlight key words in the question. Before answering a question, look for the key words. Some candidates find it useful to read through the question with a highlighter pen and pick out the key words for themselves.

| Question | | Answer | Mark |
|---|---|---|---|
| 3 | | LAN Local Area Network | 1 |
| | | WAN Wide Area Network | 1 |

**Examiner's tip** Do not try to guess this type of question and remember you must have exactly the right technical terms to gain marks.

| Question | | Answer | Mark |
|---|---|---|---|
| 4 | | 'Fly by wire' means that the pilot uses a computer input device, rather | 1 |
| | | than manual mechanically linked controls to instruct a computer to | 1 |
| | | control the output devices, for example flaps and other mechanical | 2 |
| | | devices. This type of system helps to monitor and correct any pilot error | 1 |
| | | and also lightens the amount of force needed on the controls. | 1 |

**Examiner's tip** This type of question is aimed at testing your ability to relate what you have learned to a real context. If you think about the question and its relationship to control systems, you should be able to make a good guess at the answer. Put in a practical example if you can.

| Question | | Answer | Mark |
|---|---|---|---|
| 5 | (a) | Any one of the following:<br>Hard disk/magnetic optical disk/tape drive/read-write optical disk/<br>zip and zap drive. | 1 |
| | (b) | CD ROM | 1 |
| | (c) | Write Once Read Many Times | 1 |

**Examiner's tip** Each question is worth a single mark, but you must use the correct terminology, so in (b) CD would not gain a mark. CD ROM is the correct computing term.

| | | | |
|---|---|---|---|
| | (d) | RAM is volatile; ROM is non-volatile. The user can change RAM contents,<br>but cannot change ROM contents. ROM is used to hold the operating<br>system/BIOS. RAM is used to hold the user's programs and data. | 2<br>1<br>1 |

**Examiner's tip** The last part of questions is usually the hardest, particularly on higher tier papers. This question contains four parts: what is ROM, what is RAM, and for each give an example. It is very easy to miss out part of the answer and lose valuable marks.

| | | | |
|---|---|---|---|
| 6 | | Bus network with spurs. | 2 |

**Examiner's tip** It is easy to miss the spurs, two marks can be awarded in this question and this gives you a clue.

| | | | |
|---|---|---|---|
| 7 | | The software puts questions up on the screen. The child keys in an<br>answer. If the answer is correct, the system congratulates the child,<br>often with a smiling face or some other graphic that encourages the<br>child. Depending on how many answers the child gets right, the<br>program progresses to more difficult sums. If the child gets the answer<br>wrong, the system sets easier sums. | 2<br>1<br>1<br>1<br><br>1 |

**Examiner's tip** For maximum marks, you must explain each stage of the process and how the software interacts with the child. Your answer should be in a logical order and explain what happens when the child gets sums right or wrong.

## 2 WORD PROCESSING

| Question | Answer | Mark |
|---|---|---|
| 1 (a) | Kearan had forgotten to save his work at regular intervals.<br>OR He had forgotten to set 'autosave' to save the work automatically. | 2 |

**Examiner's tip** Look at the mark allocation. Where more than one mark is allocated the examiner wants more than a one-word answer. You would get one mark for 'save work', but two for the full answer.

| Question | Answer | Mark |
|---|---|---|
| (b) | AutoSave is a software feature, whereby you can tell the software to save the work for you automatically (for example, every 4 minutes). | 2 |

**Examiner's tip** Often questions with more than one part contain clues to the answers in the first part; for example AutoSave gives a clue to the answer in 1(a) that the problem is due to lack of saved text. Look out for these clues. They can help you to gain marks.

| Question | Answer | Mark |
|---|---|---|
| (c) | The first time you save a new document, you use 'save as' and the software will ask what name you want to save the document under. | 1 |
| | Each time you save the document after that, the 'save' command will | 1 |
| | overwrite the original document. If you want to retain the original | 1 |
| | document and also save a new version, you must use the 'save as' command, and the new version will then have to be given a different name. | 1 |

**Examiner's tip** Where the question has two parts, for example 'save' and 'save as' the examiner will be looking for an explanation of both terms.

| Question | Answer | Mark |
|---|---|---|
| (d) (i) | In the computer. | 1 |
| (ii) | Through a sensor in the printer | 1 |
| | which generates a signal which is detected by the computer. | 1 |

**Examiner's tip** Often questions with a number of parts change context. In this case the word-processing question asks a control question. Look out for these changes in the latter part of long questions.

| Question | Answer | Mark |
|---|---|---|
| 2 | **A** Fully justified | 1 |
| | **B** Justified left | 1 |
| | **C** Centre justified | 1 |
| | **D** Justified right | 1 |

| Question | Answer | Mark |
|---|---|---|

**Examiner's tip** Make sure the examiner knows which term refers to which drawing and if you only know one term it is worth repeating it on all of the drawings – it will be right at least once!

| | | |
|---|---|---|
| 3 | Use of standardised letters with mail merge facilities, spelling and grammar checking, greater flexibility in choice of typefaces and layouts used. | 3<br>3 |

**Examiner's tip** Read the question carefully. It asks for three ways. Do not repeat yourself and remember the context is 'a school office'. Give examples if you can, for example mail merge could be used to send individualised standard letters to the parents.

| | | |
|---|---|---|
| 4 | Mail merge utilises a file of clients' names and addresses and merges these with a standard letter to produce individualised letters automatically. One of the most common uses of mail merge is in the junk mail we receive through our letterboxes. | 2<br>1<br>1 |

**Examiner's tip** There are two parts to this question, make sure that you answer both.

| | | |
|---|---|---|
| 5 (a) | She can add the name to the user dictionary. | 1 |

**Examiner's tip** The key word in this question is 'best' friend. If Chloë is writing a large number of letters, she will want to modify the dictionary to avoid the error message. Although 'not using the spell checker' is a viable way of achieving the desired outcome the examiner will always be looking for an IT solution, after all it is an IT examination.

| | | |
|---|---|---|
| (b) | She would ignore the message resulting from a postcode. | 1 |
| (c) | It would add unnecessary data to the user dictionary. | 1 |

**Examiner's tip** The examiner has given you a clue in (b) by suggesting it should be a different course of action.

| Question | Answer | Mark |
|---|---|---|
| (d) | Save a document template in which the style, format and type are pre-set or construct a standard for modification and saving as a new document to suit each particular letter required. | 2 |

**Examiner's tip** You must mention 'document template' or 'standard letter' to gain marks in this question.

| Question | Answer | Mark |
|---|---|---|
| 6 (a) | Change 1: Moving address to the centre of the letter.<br>Feature used: Centred text command. | 2 |
| | Change 2: Justifying the text so that the left and right borders are parallel.<br>Feature used: Justify text command. | 2 |
| | Change 3: Changing the font of the date of the letter.<br>Feature used: Format text command. | 2 |

**Examiner's tip** Look carefully at the letters to spot the changes before you attempt to answer the question. Sometimes there will be more than one change in a single part of the letter, for example text could be centred and have its font changed, or be made bold.

(b)

> 16 Springfield Close,
> Warringfield,
> Durham
>
> 19th July 1997
>
> Dear <title> <surname>,
>
> With reference to your account with us, number <account>, we regret to inform you that you appear not to have paid the amount of <amount> outstanding at the end of June.
>
> Please pay this as soon as possible. If you have paid the amount in the last few days, please ignore this letter.
>
> We look forward to hearing from you.
>
> Yours sincerely
>
> M. Counter
> Accounts

One mark for each correctly underlined section. **3**

**Examiner's tip** Underline all of the sections that appear inside the mail merge markers.

| Question | Answer | Mark |
|---|---|---|
| 7 | Advantages: Electronic mail is instant. | 1 |
| | It can be sent worldwide. | 1 |
| | It is cheaper than conventional mail as it uses less paper and costs only a local telephone call. | 1 |
| | Disadvantages: Each recipient needs to have a mail box and a computer system (the computer must be switched on and the user must log on). | 1 |
| | There is a lack of privacy. | 1 |
| | You do not have a paper copy to refer to, unless you print it out yourself. | 1 |

**Examiner's tip** Put your answers in sentences and try to give examples. The question asks for advantage**s** and disadvantage**s** so try to give more than one answer in each case. In this instance the examiner wants three advantages and three disadvantages. It does not say this in the question, but you can tell from the number of marks to be awarded.

## 3 DATABASES

| Question | Answer | Mark |
|---|---|---|
| 1 (a) | Any four of the following: Married/three children/secretary/home owner/£40 000 mortgage/credit card/reads books. | 4 |

**Examiner's tip** With this type of question you need to think back to the sort of data you have put into a database. There are only four marks for four statements so short answers will suffice.

| Question | Answer | Mark |
|---|---|---|
| (b) | Data has no context. | 1 |
| | Information is data in a context. | 1 |

**Examiner's tip** The question asks for an explanation, so write a complete sentence. Make sure you answer both parts of the question. It is easy to fill the space with a half complete answer.

| Question | | Answer | Mark |
|---|---|---|---|
| 2 | (a) | A distributed database is used on networks of several computers, | 2 |
| | | with each computer sharing part of the data and co-operating in | 1 |
| | | making it available to the user. | 1 |
| | (b) | In a relational database data is stored in a series of tables, each linked | 2 |
| | | to each other by the database management system. This enables the | |
| | | user to view the data in a variety of ways and allows more flexibility | 1 |
| | | in terms of data access and type of query. | 1 |

**Examiner's tip** Do not waffle. Each part has been awarded four marks. This indicates that the examiner is looking for a high level of response. If possible, give examples of use to demonstrate your depth of knowledge. If you do not know the answer, leave the question until you have finished the other questions rather than spending time on irrelevant answers.

3

| Field Name | Length | Field Type | Mark |
|---|---|---|---|
| Date | 8 | Date | 1 |
| First Name | 12 | Alpha-numeric | 1 |
| Surname | 12 | Alpha-numeric | 1 |
| Boy-Girl | 1 | True/false | 1 |
| Age | 2 | Numeric | 1 |
| Address | 18 | Alpha-numeric | 1 |

**Examiner's tip** You must use the correct terminology for the software you use and do not simply state alpha-numeric in all of the fields.

| Question | | Answer | Mark |
|---|---|---|---|
| 4 | (a) | Alphabetically upon surname. | 1 |
| | (b) | There are not 31 days in February. | 1 |

**Examiner's tip** This is a very common type of question where the examiner will put a deliberate mistake in a database or spreadsheet for you to find. Look carefully, but remember it is only worth one mark. Do not spend too much time finding it.

| Question | | Answer | Mark |
|---|---|---|---|
| | (c) | Make the field a date field, not an alpha-numeric field. | 1 |
| | (d) | Any reasonable response gains a mark with one extra mark for the use of the syntax >. E.g. DATE=>01/01/1994 and SEX=M. | 3 |

| Question | Answer | Mark |
|---|---|---|

**Examiner's tip** Remember to use the correct syntax for any database search questions.

| | | |
|---|---|---|
| (e) | The field length is the number of characters or numbers that can be typed into the field. | 1 |
| (f) | A true/false field can hold a single letter or number to indicate whether the value in the field is true or false. | 1 |

**Examiner's tip** Where the question asks for a statement worth a single mark, give a very brief description, for example a single sentence.

| | | |
|---|---|---|
| 5 (a) | A field which uniquely identifies a record. | 1 |
| (b) | Reference. | 1 |

**Examiner's tip** Even if you used this information in the previous section, for example 'A field which uniquely identifies a record, for example in this database it is the Reference field', give the answer again. Do not expect the examiner to notice that you have answered the question correctly in the wrong place.

| | | |
|---|---|---|
| (c) | 002, 005 and 006. | 1 |
| (d) | No. | 1 |

**Examiner's tip** This type of question is set to see if you understand the structure of a database and can read information from one. Remember to use the exact field names shown in the sample database and give the correct numbers. Failure to do so can cost marks.

| | | |
|---|---|---|
| (e) (i) | Supplier Reference, | 1 |
| | B004. | 1 |
| (ii) | Stock < Min Level AND Replace = Y<br>One mark for each component:<br>Stock, <, Min level, AND, Replace, =, Y. | 7 |

**Examiner's tip** Where large numbers of marks have been allocated for this type of question, the marks have been split up so that each piece of the search formula has been give a mark. Make sure you read the question carefully and state the exact formula using the full names of the fields and the correct query language.

| Question | | Answer | Mark |
|---|---|---|---|
| 6 | (a) | *Reference.* | 1 |
| | (b) | *True/false.* | 1 |

**Examiner's tip** The library must have a unique number for each book and it can only be in or out.

| Question | | Answer | Mark |
|---|---|---|---|
| | (c) | *Delete books that are old, destroyed, stolen or lost.* | 1 |
| | | *Carry out a regular stock check.* | 1 |
| | | *Make sure every book that leaves the library is entered into the database to prevent theft.* | 1 |
| | | *Check that all the books taken are entered correctly.* | 1 |

**Examiner's tip** The question asks for steps, so the examiner wants more than one key action.

| Question | | Answer | Mark |
|---|---|---|---|
| | (d) | *Date.* | 1 |
| | (e) | One of the following in each case: | |
| | | Advantages for the librarian: *Speed of booking out/in books/automatic records/ease of use.* | 2 |
| | | Disadvantages for the school: *Cost of equipment/need for staff training/Need to add bar codes to books.* | 2 |

**Examiner's tip** The question does not state who you are considering as the main user, so you can choose the school, the librarian or the borrower. Give a full description and add an example of why it is an advantage or disadvantage.

# 4 spreadsheets

| Question | | Answer | Mark |
|---|---|---|---|
| 1 | (a) | D5 = B5*C5 | 1 |
| | | C7 = SUM(C2:C6) OR = C2+C3+C4+C5+C6 | 1 |
| | | D7 = SUM(D2:D6) OR = D2+D3+D4+D5+D6 (1 extra for 'SUM') | 2 |

**Examiner's tip** Be careful to give the correct formula and use abbreviations and functions where they are appropriate. For example, for totals you will get marks for = C2+C3+C4+C5+C6, but you will get an extra mark if you use the function SUM(). The examiner will be looking for your knowledge of functions.

| Question | | Answer | Mark |
|---|---|---|---|
| | (b) | Advantage 1: The spreadsheet automatically does the calculations | 1 |
| | | for the user and when the sales totals are changed, the spreadsheet recalculates automatically, | 1 |
| | | Advantage 2: It is quick and easy to use and the operator always | 1 |
| | | knows the total sales. | 1 |

**Examiner's tip** Give a full explanation and remember to use all of the lines provided. Try to make your answers specific to the question – the key word in this question is 'formula'. The examiner is looking for the advantages of building formula into a spreadsheet.

| Question | | Answer | Mark |
|---|---|---|---|
| | (c) | = (B5-E5)C5 | 2 |

**Examiner's tip** The advantage of a spreadsheet is that you do not need to do manual calculations. Examiners will increase the level of difficulty through a question. This section requires a more complex formula than before, do not simply put in the answer from a manual calculation. The calculation must be automatic when any of the variables are changed.

| Question | | Answer | Mark |
|---|---|---|---|
| | (d) | Through the use of Dynamic Data Exchange (DDE) or Object Link Embedding (OLE). | 4 |

**Examiner's tip** Where you are asked to describe a process towards the end of a question, think of each step you must carry out. Try to explain what type of link you are setting up. Use the correct specialist terms as well as the correct process. Show the examiner what you know, understand and can do.

| Question | | Answer | Mark |
|---|---|---|---|
| 2 | (a) | Formula: = (B4*C4)+D4+E4 | 2 |
| | (b) | Method: Using the copy command. | 2 |
| | (c) | Formula: = Sum(F4:F8) | 2 |

**Examiner's tip** Note there is an extra mark in (c) for using the function SUM(). You would have gained one mark only had you answered = F4+F5+F6+F7+F8.

| Question | | Answer | Mark |
|---|---|---|---|
| | (d) | A computer model will allow the restaurant to experiment with various options, for example: | |
| | | reduced portions to reduce the costs of ingredients, | 2 |
| | | larger batch sizes to reduce overheads and, thus, the cost per unit, | 2 |
| | | larger batch sizes to reduce unit costs of ingredients, | 2 |
| | | lower pay for the other chef. | 2 |

**Examiner's tip** A full explanation is required, showing that you understand that a computer model allows you to experiment with various options. Try to make your answers specific to the question – the model allows for a large number of variables. Try to use all of them.

| Question | | Answer | Mark |
|---|---|---|---|
| 3 | (a) | Information 1: Name of customer. | 1 |
| | | Information 2: Address of customer. | 1 |
| | (b) | | |

| Name | Address | Product | Product Price | Number | Total Cost | Unique Customer Reference number |
|---|---|---|---|---|---|---|
| | | | | | | |
| | | | | | | |
| | | | | | | |
| | | | | | | |

(1 mark for each heading to a maximum of 6) **6**

**Examiner's tip** Read the question and show how you would include all the fields given, alongside the extra fields needed to show information you have stated are necessary in 3(a).

| Question | Answer | Mark |
|---|---|---|
| (c) | The total cost of the goods purchased could be automatically added up using a formula. By inserting Product Codes automatic prices would be included in the spreadsheet and totals would link to the customer reference. | 2<br>1 |

**Examiner's tip** The description must relate to your own design for a spreadsheet and should show how various items purchased are linked together as a single customer record.The key to this part of the question is to link the various items together in a single invoice for each customer.

| Question | Answer | Mark |
|---|---|---|
| (d) | Marks will be awarded according to the spreadsheet designed for correct formula using the correct syntax. E.g.:<br>F2=D2xE2 for each row with Customer Reference in column G. | 4 |
| 4 | A spreadsheet allows you to change one cell and affect the content of a large number of other cells. A spreadsheet can produce diagrams and charts to help you make your choice. You can use a spreadsheet to ask 'what if' questions and test hypotheses. You can use a spreadsheet for statistical analysis. | 1<br>2<br>1<br>2 |

**Examiner's tip** You will not receive marks for general answers. You must specifically state how the spreadsheet could be used to help model the costs and compare alternatives.

| Question | Answer | Mark |
|---|---|---|
| 5 | Analysis of the situation.<br>Design of solutions.<br>Implementation of system.<br>Training and trials.<br>Evaluation of the system. | 1<br>1<br>1<br>1<br>1 |

**Examiner's tip** The stages that you go through in designing and implementing a system are the same whatever the context. Make sure you put the stages in the right order.

# 5 CONTROL SYSTEMS

| Question | Answer | Mark |
|---|---|---|
| 1 | Pen down; Forward 50; Turn left 90; Forward 50; Turn left 90;<br>Forward 50; Turn left 90; Forward 50; Pen up. | 3<br>2 |

**Examiner's tip** You must use the exact instructions given in the table. Do not write anything other than the commands required. You could turn left or right.

| Question | Answer | Mark |
|---|---|---|
| 2 | Any two of the following:<br>Timer/temperature cutout/door sensor to switch on light/temperature setting. | 2 |

**Examiner's tip** Make sure you do not describe the same device twice using different words.

| Question | Answer | Mark |
|---|---|---|
| 3 | In monitoring traffic/in monitoring a scientific experiment. | 1 |

**Examiner's tip** Do not simply repeat the example given. Be careful to ensure that your answer is a data logging device and not a manually controlled input device, such as a bar code reader.

| Question | Answer | Mark |
|---|---|---|
| 4 | Optical sensor/bumper connected to a microswitch/sonar. | 3 |

**Examiner's tip** Make sure you read the question correctly. The sensor required does not follow the white line.

| Question | Answer | Mark |
|---|---|---|
| 5 | Any three of the following:<br>To monitor experiments, for example data logging/to keep records of files and equipment/to model dangerous situations/to word process and record the results of experiments/to simulate experiments and control conditions. | 3 |

**Examiner's tip** Questions which ask for a description require answers of more than one word. The number of lines indicated on the examination paper gives a clear indication of the length of response required.

| Question | Answer | Mark |
|---|---|---|
| 6 | Central heating, traffic lights. | 2 |

**Examiner's tip** Your first instincts are usually the best on multiple choice questions.

| Question | Answer | Mark |
|---|---|---|
| 7 (a) | The infrared beams are broken in a particular sequence, which tells the control system whether a car is entering or leaving the car park. | 2 |
| (b) | Watch the cars entering or leaving the car park and check that the system is functioning correctly. Check when the car park is empty/full that the system states that it is empty/full. | 2 |
| (c) | Limitation 1: If two cars entered side by side or too close to each other end to end, they would be counted as only one car. | 1 |
| | Correction 1: Redesign the entrance to the car park so that only one car can enter at a time. | 1 |
| | Limitation 2: People could walk past the infrared beams and be counted as a car. | 1 |
| | Correction 2: Do not count the number of cars unless both infrared beams are broken at the same time. | 1 |

**Examiner's tip** Make sure that you do not repeat the same answers more than once, using different words, as you will only receive the marks for an answer once. Use technical terms where they are appropriate.

## 6 DESKTOP PUBLISHING

| Question | Answer | Mark |
|---|---|---|
| 1 (a) | Any two of the following:<br>Modem link to telephone/load software/dial up number/type in access code/type password/load text file and transmit. | 2 |

**Examiner's tip** In this type of question you must show your knowledge by stating the equipment requirements, for example telephone and modem.

| Question | Answer | Mark |
|---|---|---|
| (b) | For example, you could import the text from the article and import scanned or photographed TIF images into the text, change the font, layout, colour and create frames. | 2<br>1<br>1 |

| Question | Answer | Mark |
|---|---|---|

**Examiner's tip** This type of question requires short sentences that clearly show how to change basic text into a magazine article. You must read the question clearly and state how you could add pictures as well as the text. Try to be concise in your answer and add technical terms where appropriate.

| Question | Answer | Mark |
|---|---|---|
| 2 (a) | Use: To draw common shapes accurately, for example polygons, squares, rectangles and circles. | 1 |
| (b) | Use: To fill enclosed shapes with colours, tints or shades. | 1 |
| (c) | Use: To select colour, tint or shade for use with fill command or other drawing tools. | 1 |
| (d) | Use: To add words and labels. | 1 |
| (e) | Use: To allow you to draw shapes that are irregular or not available in the pre-set selection. | 1 |
| (f) | Use: To rotate drawings or text blocks. | 1 |

**Examiner's tip** Think about the actions that are described, as the question might not use the same commands as the software packages with which you are familiar. The examiner will select terms that describe common software features. You are not expected to be used to every available kind of software.

3

**Clip-art** is freely available, is copyright free, is easy to access and contains a large amount of pre-drawn material. Its disadvantages are that lots of other people will have used the same images, and the Clip-art may not contain the exact picture you want. 1 1

**Drawing your own images** means that you have exactly the image you want, but you need to be skilled at drawing, and it could take a long time. 1 1

**Scanning** images has the advantage that you can copy material from any source, so there is a very large amount of resource to draw on. The disadvantages are the cost of scanners, the size of your computer memory, and the possibility that you could break the law by using a copyrighted image. 2 1 1

**Examiner's tip** The question asks you to compare alternative methods. Therefore, you must give at least two methods and, for each, you need to state both the advantages and disadvantages of using that method.

# 7 INFORMATION SYSTEMS IN SOCIETY

| Question | | Answer | Mark |
|---|---|---|---|
| 1 | (a) | Yes. | 1 |
| | (b) | It would be legal for Alpha to sell the data provided that the company had registered under the Act that it intended to sell the data. | 2 |

**Examiner's tip** The second part of the question asks when it would be legal for Alpha to sell the data. Always read a question carefully because it may contain a clue to the answer. The way that this question is worded gives you a clue that it would be legal for Alpha to sell the data under *certain* circumstances. You must describe these circumstances clearly.

| Question | | Answer | Mark |
|---|---|---|---|
| 2 | (a) | Any three of the following:<br>Age/allergies/weight/details of immunisations/details of past illnesses/addictions/contraceptives used. | 3 |
| | (b) | By having a password or encryption, and keeping computer files secure, for example locking the room the computer is in, barring the windows and installing an alarm system. | 2 |
| | (c) | Yes. | 1 |

**Examiner's tip** Exam boards like to ask questions about places that we use regularly, such as doctor's surgeries and banks. Despite the fact that these services are often vital parts of our everyday lives and may not seem the same as commercial companies, they still have to obey the laws about data protection.

| Question | | Answer | Mark |
|---|---|---|---|
| 3 | | Statements could be delivered to the wrong address. Money could be | 2 |
| | | credited to the wrong account. You could be told you were overdrawn | 1 |
| | | when you weren't. People could draw your money out by mistake or intent. | 1 |

**Examiner's tip** The examiner is always looking for more than one example, but be careful not to say the same thing in a different way.

| Question | | Answer | Mark |
|---|---|---|---|
| 4 | (a) | Way 1: Monitoring known criminals. | 1 |
| | | Way 2: Patrolling 'black spots' (areas where there is a lot of crime). | 1 |
| | (b) | Way 1: Matching fingerprint samples. | 1 |
| | | Way 2: DNA profiles and information on suspects' past movements. | 1 |

**Examiner's tip** Do not put the same answers for both parts of the question. Make sure that the suggestions you make would result from computer-stored data.

| Question | Answer | Mark |
|---|---|---|
| **5** (a) | A bar code | **1** |
| | is scanned. | **1** |

**Examiner's tip** Two marks are possible so the answer must be more than one word.

| Question | Answer | Mark |
|---|---|---|
| (b) | Each item will be a record in a computer file in the main computer. | **2** |

**Examiner's tip** Remember that a shop will use a mainframe computer and the tills are simply terminals.

| Question | Answer | Mark |
|---|---|---|
| (c) | Any two of the following:<br>It will be faster through the checkout, which will lead to shorter queues. There will be fewer mistakes and better stock control, which should prevent the shop from running out of items. It will give me a fully itemised shopping bill. | **4** |
| (d) | Any two of the following:<br>There is no need to pay staff to put price labels on every item. The manager will be able to monitor the performance of individual checkout staff. Fewer checkout staff will be required. There is less chance of an error at the checkout. Automatic stock control. | **4** |

**Examiner's tip** Even if there are similar benefits to both manager and customers, do not list the same benefit twice. Examiners are looking for different answers for each part. This type of question can usually be answered from general knowledge or DOS systems. Imagine the differences between shops of today and shops before computerisation and guess the answers if you are not sure of a response.

| Question | Answer | Mark |
|---|---|---|
| **6** (a) | Any three of the following:<br>The data must be obtained lawfully and fairly.<br>It must be kept secure.<br>It should be destroyed when no longer required.<br>It must not be excessive.<br>You must be allowed to see any data kept on you, on request.<br>The shop must register and use the data only for registered purposes. | **3** |

**Examiner's tip** General knowledge answers will not gain marks on this type of question. As the question **specifically** refers to the **Data Protection Act** your answers must do the same. If a question refers to a specific law, do not give general knowledge answers.

| Question | Answer | Mark |
|---|---|---|
| (b) | Any three of the following:<br>Word processed documents/data stored on paper/data stored for wage purpose/data where the individual cannot be identified/data held for personal purposes/data about members of private clubs where all members have agreed to store the data. | 3 |

**Examiner's tip** Think about the types of data that are stored and where you do not need to apply for registration.

| Question | Answer | Mark |
|---|---|---|
| 7 (a) | Any sensible reasons would be allowed – one mark for brief responses and two marks for expanded points.<br>Way 1: Access to other people's research papers. | 2 |
| | Way 2: Can use the web to send out questions and make contact with experts. | 2 |

**Examiner's tip** Think about the Internet and its use as a communications system. A researcher needs access to information.

| Question | Answer | Mark |
|---|---|---|
| (b) (i) | To prevent illegal material being available. To control pornographic and other unsuitable material. To avoid the illegal transfer of copyright material. To stop libel. To control terrorists. | 2<br>1<br>1 |
| (ii) | The Internet provides a freely available source of information. Private mail should not be censored. Censorship could be on political grounds. It is difficult to enforce and costly to incorporate. | 1<br>2<br>1 |

**Examiner's tip** Where questions are given this many marks the examiner usually wants more than one reason, even where this is not stated in the question.

| Question | Answer | Mark |
|---|---|---|
| 8 (a) | Any two of the following:<br>Less chance of error/automatic data entry/speed. | 2 |
| (b) | Any two of the following:<br>The item code/price/manufacturer/date/country of origin. | 2 |

**Examiner's tip** The best way to answer this question is to think of what types of output are required to produce an automatic bill and re-order the goods.

| Question | Answer | Mark |
|---|---|---|
| (c) (ii) | There is a bleep or flashing light. | 1 |
| (ii) | Key in the number by hand from the number displayed under the bar code. | 1 |

| Question | Answer | Mark |
|---|---|---|

**Examiner's tip** This question is based upon a supermarket checkout. It is not asking for specific computer knowledge, only general knowledge about the use of systems.

| Question | Answer | Mark |
|---|---|---|
| 9 (a) | A virus is a piece of software that corrupts other software and is transmitted from one computer to another. | 2 |

**Examiner's tip** You need to give a full answer and state what the virus does (corrupts) and in what form the virus is (software).

| Question | Answer | Mark |
|---|---|---|
| (b) | Any two of the following:<br>Do not let anyone use discs. Scan the discs first using a dedicated anti-virus machine. Use anti-virus software or a virus scanner. | 2 |

**Examiner's tip** Your school will have a way of dealing with this problem. Simply state what this is.

## 8 MOCK EXAMINATION PAPER

| Question | Answer | | Mark |
|---|---|---|---|
| 1 (b) | **Device** | **Type of device input/output** | |
| | touch pad | Input | |
| | monitor | Output | |
| | keyboard | Input | |
| | laser printer | Output | |
| | video camera | Input (one mark per correct answer.) | 5 |
| (b) | Award one mark for each correct answer:<br>Sharing expensive output/input devices e.g. plotters, printers, hard drives, video camera.<br>Ability to share data.<br>Share software.<br>Improved communication between dentist and receptionist. | | 3 |
| (c) | Local area network. | | 1 |
| (d) | Wide area network. | | 1 |
| 2 (a) (i) | Primary Field: Last name. | | 1 |
| | Secondary Field: First name. | | 1 |
| (ii) | In the DoB field the year is incorrect for David Yeomans. | | 2 |

Letts Q&A

| Question | | Answer | Mark |
|---|---|---|---|
| | (iii) | **Field** — **Type of Field**<br>Last Name — Alpha/numeric<br>Address — Alpha/numeric<br>Post Code — Alpha/numeric<br>DoB — numeric | 4 |
| | (iv) | A field that can only have two values: true/false. | 1 |
| | (v) | The number of characters allowed for in a field. | 1 |
| | (vi) | Last Apt (one mark only), or Last Apt = <01/03/99 | 2 |
| (b) | | <First Name> <Last Name><br><Address><br><Post Code><br><br>Dear <First Name><br>You are due for a dental check-up. Please contact our office on 01432 888888 to make an appropriate appointment.<br>Yours sincerely<br><br><Dentist> | 4 |
| (c) | (i) | Data Protection Act.<br>1984 | 1<br>1 |
| | (ii) | 1 mark each for any three of the following:<br>ensure accuracy of data,<br>let individuals see their own data on request,<br>sign a public register,<br>collect the data in a fair way. | 3 |
| | (iii) | 1 mark each for any two of the following:<br>password, encryption, security in the building, fire walls on the system, secure storage. | 2 |
| 3 (a) | | =(C4/D4)*E4 | 1 |
| (b) | | =F2+F3+F4+F5 (one mark only), or =Sum(F2:F5) | 2 |
| (c) | | Your answer should include most of the following points:<br>To identify the supplier, help in searching for stock items, useful in stock checking, easy to include in other databases and spreadsheets, helps identify a stock item even if you are not a dental expert, avoids confusion between two similar items. | 1<br>2<br><br>1 |
| 4 (a) | | Your answer should include most of the following points:<br>An intranet is a private network only for use between the dentists in the group. The internet provides access to the world wide network. | 3<br>1 |
| (b) | | The dental practice could create its own web pages and provide valuable information on dental hygiene to attract potential customers. | 2 |

| Question | | Answer | Mark |
|---|---|---|---|
| (c) | | Up to 2 marks for each well articulated reason. This could include: | |
| | | The ability to keep up to date and carry out research, | 2 |
| | | the use of newsgroups to communicate with dental colleagues | 1 |
| | | around the world, access to government information and medical database, | 1 |
| | | could use video conferencing facilities, | 1 |
| | | could use it to order stock. | 1 |
| (d) | (i) | A number of answers is possible. Up to two marks for one advantage and two for one disadvantage. For example: | |
| | | Advantages: It is much quicker than conventional post and is cheaper to send | 2 |
| | | Disadvantages: you have to have expensive equipment and someone could intercept your personal mail. If you live in an area without good telecommunications or electricity, or if the people you send letters to do not have e-mail, then e-mail is of no use to you. | 2 |
| | (ii) | You could use a camera and send pictures, attach documents and save money if communicating abroad, as e-mail is a local call away. | 2 |
| | | Telephones are, however, easier to gain access to, can contact more people at present and can be perceived as being more friendly. | 2 |